Advance Praise for "Riding the Current"

"In choosing this topic for her book Madelyn shows how her finger is clearly on the pulse of the challenges of the knowledge worker of the 21st Century."
   –Denise Lee, Senior Knowledge Management Consultant, PricewaterhouseCoopers.

"Madelyn Blair leads us on a fascinating journey with many unexpected twists and turns. Along the way, we get a multitude of tools, techniques and insights to help keep our knowledge fresh."
   –Steve Denning, author of *The Leader's Guide to Storytelling* and *The Secret of Language of Leadership*.

"This book is a real addition to anyone's knowledge management, adult learning or appreciative inquiry library. The topic of personal knowledge management is uniquely presented here with an accessible framework, application guides and tips, stories from practitioners, and a look over the author's shoulder as she practices what she preaches."
   – Craig DeLarge, Associate Director, Nova Nordisk

"This book is a must-read for anyone who takes his or her self-development seriously. *Riding the Current* lays out technique after technique for staying abreast of everything that is relevant, navigating the overwhelming sea of knowledge, and using it all to your advantage."
   – Seth Kahan, VisionaryLeadership.com, author of **Fast Co's** expert blog, *Leading Change*

"Among all the knowledge management books one is unlikely to find such practical wisdom based on hands on experience, written for audiences of all ages and at all stages of life – the art of self improvement turned into practical science. Congratulations!"
   –Uma Lele, Senior Advisor, World Bank Independent Evaluation Department.

"A few years ago, as my children grew and became more independent, I set out on a voyage I had always dreamed of taking: that of learning to write stories, to craft beautiful novels of the type I have always loved reading. There is a tremendous learning curve from being a passionate reader to being a skilled novelist. I devoured every lesson I could lay eyes or ears on, from books and articles about craft to classes, workshops, and conferences – and sometimes felt myself lost in a jungle of information, much of it contradictory! Since beginning this journey, I have struggled to carry the unwieldy mass of advice forward with me. The insights in *Riding the Current* have provided me with a new perspective on my goals and learning needs. Instead of feeling overwhelmed by the amount of advice I had learned and the amount of knowledge I felt I had yet to learn, I see the endless opportunities in daily life and writing practice to keep my knowledge fresh. The words of masters and teachers are only one avenue of knowledge. To someone with an open and curious mind, the entire world is teacher. I have gone from counting the endless steps required to climb this mountain, to taking in the beautiful views as I climb."
> – **Beth Flannery**, author and mother.

"Learning something new is the ultimate magic experience. How learning becomes knowledge, both personal and organizational has been studied, dissected and debated for many years. Madelyn Blair has crafted a book that unlocks the magic for individuals and organizations wishing to increase their ability to find knowledge in the sea of information we are bombarded with daily. Madelyn is first and foremost a master story crafter. Her unique ability to move through the English language with selective precision allows her to explain learning with the clarity one only finds on a spring day after an early morning rain storm. By illustrating her thoughts with rich personal anecdotes and stories, she creates a template for learning that any organization or individual can rapidly apply to their own environment with maximum impact. This book is truly a must read for 'Seekers of new knowledge' and those wishing to keep their knowledge fresh and relevant."
> – **Peter J.Engstrom**, Board Chairman, At Home Chesapeake, and former Chief Knowledge Officer for Federal Business, Science Applications International Corporation (SAIC).

"Madelyn is a gracious host of insights. Don't pass up a seat at her masterfully prepared feast. Stories will tickle your palate and you will be drawn into a delicious conversation. Taste the principles and practices that transform our performances. Share a copy with others and secure your spot in the Hall of Fame for life long learners."
> –**Terrence Gargiulo**, President, MAKINGSTORIES.net, author, *The Strategic Use of Stories in Organizational Communication & Learning*

"If you are looking to effectively build your 'knowledge backbone,' look no further. Madelyn will give you the tools and practices to hone your knowledge edge and enjoy the journey!"
> – **Jacqueline Kelm**, Founder of Appreciative Living, LLC & author of The Joy of Appreciative Living.

"Madelyn Blair has written a timely and provocative book. Her insights into how we learn as well the importance of a practice partner resonate with me as a consultant to people in the not for profit, faith based organization. Often these practice partners are found outside our own disciplines and as Madelyn writes that in choosing them, 'We open white space, we expose assumptions and we reveal more areas to explore in our learning.' Madelyn's emphasis on the relational in learning supports what many may know instinctively. Indeed, her work is common sense subjected to her personal reflection and own rigorous discipline. It is an excellent book. Only one caution: it should be read only by those serious in the desire to keep learning fresh and alive! I highly recommend it for those on the journey of life long formation and education."
> – **Brenda Hermann**, MSBT ACSW

"Learning how to learn is the greatest gift you can teach yourself. *Riding the Current* is a powerful primer for how to translate your knowledge into meaningful value. In this new adaptive age, everybody needs to know how to manage and understand what they know. Blair's book provides an insightful personal field guide - with a wealth of concepts to guide you on this important journey."
> – **Michael Margolis**, President of Get Storied, and Author, *Believe Me: Why Your Vision, Brand, and Leadership Need a Bigger Story*

"Madelyn Blair has written the book I needed 12 years ago when I stumbled out of corporate life and into making my own way. Luckily for me, for much of that time she's been a friend and I've been privileged to have conversations with her as she has gathered her life experience and rendered it into wisdom to help others. This is a dangerously easy read, and could lure you into thinking that it's an easy book because of that. It isn't and its value lies in drawing you in and hooking you before you realize it. The mix of personal reminiscence and reflection, insights shared by her interviews and really practical steps of discovery that each reader can choose to take at their own pace makes for a book which is more of a journey than a read, and the better for it. The deceptive simplicity of the suggestions, not always easy to follow, tells us how, in learning this profound and satisfying practice of constant self discovery and rediscovery, one must also be ready to unlearn, and Madelyn makes this possible, both in the book and in the brilliant suggestions of taking on a crew to help you. The possibilities on the roles of Accompanier and Practice Partner do much to repair the fabric of work life and provide necessary ballast and support to many people, whether freelancers or in employment, who increasingly feel isolated and disconnected in a work context. Permission to ask for companionship on the journey is perhaps the single most important idea in this book, and one that should be considered by everyone."

-**Victoria Ward,** Partner, Sparknow.

Riding the Current

How to deal with the daily deluge of data

by Madelyn
Blair, PhD

illustrations by Nusa Maal

Taos Institute Publications, 2010

RIDING THE CURRENT:
HOW TO DEAL WITH THE DAILY DELUGE OF DATA

FIRST EDITION
© 2010 Madelyn Blair
© 2010 COVER IMAGE by Nusa Maal

Library of Congress Catalog Card Number: 2010924013

Taos Institute Publications
A Division of the Taos Institute
Chagrin Falls, Ohio
USA

ISBN-10: 0-9819076-5-2
ISBN-13: 978-0-9819076-5-9   Printed in the USA and in the UK

Taos Institute Publications

The Taos Institute is a nonprofit organization dedicated to the development of social constructionist theory and practice for purposes of world benefit. Constructionist theory and practice locate the source of meaning, value, and action in communicative relations among people. Our major investment is in fostering relational processes that can enhance the welfare of people and the world in which they live. Taos Institute Publications offers contributions to cutting-edge theory and practice in social construction. Our books are designed for scholars, practitioners, students, and the openly curious public. The **Focus Book Series** provides brief introductions and overviews that illuminate theories, concepts, and useful practices. The **Tempo Book Series** is especially dedicated to the general public and to practitioners. The **Books for Professionals Series** provides in-depth works that focus on recent developments in theory and practice. Our books are particularly relevant to social scientists and to practitioners concerned with individual, family, organizational, community, and societal change.

Kenneth J. Gergen
President, Board of Directors
The Taos Institute

For information about the Taos Institute and social constructionism
visit: www.taosinstitute.net

Taos Institute Publications

Taos Tempo Series:Collaborative Practices for Changing Times
Ordinary Life Therapy: Experiences from a Collaborative Systemic Practice, (2009) by Carina
    Håkansson
Mapping Dialogue: Essential Tools for Social Change, (2008) by Marianne "Mille" Bojer,
    Heiko Roehl, Mariane Knuth-Hollesen, and Colleen Magner
*Positive Family Dynamics: Appreciative Inquiry Questions to Bring Out the Best in
    Families*, (2008) by Dawn Cooperrider Dole, Jen Hetzel Silbert, Ada Jo Mann,   and
    Diana Whitney

Focus Book Series
The Appreciative Organization, Revised Edition (2008) by Harlene Anderson,
    David Cooperrider, Ken Gergen, Mary Gergen, Sheila McNamee, Jane Watkins, and
    Diana Whitney
Appreciative Inquiry: A Positive Approach to Building Cooperative Capacity, (2005)
    by Frank Barrett and Ronald Fry
Dynamic Relationships: Unleashing the Power of Appreciative Inquiry in Daily Living,
    (2005) by Jacqueline Stavros and Cheri B. Torres
*Appreciative Sharing of Knowledge: Leveraging Knowledge Management for
    Strategic Change*, (2004) by Tojo Thatchekery
Social Construction: Entering the Dialogue, (2004) by Kenneth J. Gergen, and Mary Gergen
Appreciative Leaders: In the Eye of the Beholder, (2001) edited by Marge Schiller,
    Bea Mah Holland, and Deanna Riley
*Experience AI: A Practitioner's Guide to Integrating Appreciative Inquiry and
    Experiential Learning*, (2001) by Miriam Ricketts and Jim Willis

Books for Professionals Series
Positive Approaches to Peacebuilding: A Resource for Innovators, (2010) edited by Cynthia
    Sampson, Mohammed Abu-Nimer, Claudia Liebler, and Diana Whitney
Social Construction on the Edge: 'Withness'-Thinking & Embodiment, (2010) by John Shotter
Joined Imagination: Writing and Language in Therapy, (2009) by Peggy Penn
Celebrating the Other: A Dialogic Account of Human Nature, (reprint 2008) by Edward
    Sampson
Conversational Realities Revisited: Life, Language, Body and World, (2008) by John Shotter
Horizons in Buddhist Psychology: Practice, Research and Theory, (2006) edited by Maurits
    Kwee, Kenneth J. Gergen, and Fusako Koshikawa
Therapeutic Realities: Collaboration, Oppression and Relational Flow, (2005) by
    Kenneth J. Gergen
SocioDynamic Counselling: A Practical Guide to Meaning Making, (2004) by R. Vance Peavy
Experiential Exercises in Social Construction – A Fieldbook for Creating Change, (2004) by
    Robert Cottor, Alan Asher, Judith Levin, and Cindy Weiser
Dialogues About a New Psychology, (2004) by Jan Smedslund

For book information and ordering, visit Taos Institute Publications at:
www.taosinstitutepublications.net

For further information, call: 1-888-999-TAOS, 1-440-338-6733
Email: info@taosoinstitute.net

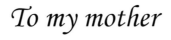

To my mother

Appreciation

Many people were willing to be interviewed as I searched for stories of how others 'ride the current.' You will meet and learn more about each of them as you read this book. Their stories make this book interesting and valuable. I appreciate every moment of their time and the stories they shared. Thank you.

Mary-Alice Arthur
Peter Block
Pedro Catarino
Freddie Ciampi
Kathy Clark
Cait Cusack
Thomas Deakins
Daniel Dixon
Fred Dogget
Molly Dogget
Raymond Douherty
David Drake
Louise Fox
Jan Gardner
Terrence Gargiulo
Kai Hagen
Dena Hawes

Christopher Heimann
Yvette Hyatter-Adams
Aram Karapetyan
Claudia L'Amoreaux
Deborah Maher
Howard Milner
Katherine Grace Morris
Laura Woods Nokes
Kat Pearl
Elaine Peresluha
Larry Prusak
Bob Sadler
Wayne Salamon
Marsha Scorza
Ralph Scorza
Rick Weldon
Rodger Whipple

Many friends and even strangers – too numerous to name – found time to lend a hand so that this book could be finished. Laura Baker who became as passionate about this book as I, added the no nonsense support every author needs. The illustrator for this book is Nusa Maal. Although her name appears on the cover, I must express gratitude for her willingness to give visual expression to my thinking and to do so unstintingly.

Thanks to all of you.

Table of Contents

Foreword

It is a great honour and pleasure to be allowed to write a few words of introduction to Madelyn Blair's new book, *Riding the Current*. I have known Madelyn for more than fifteen years now. We first met in Taos, the small town in New Mexico, where the Taos Institute, then still in its inception, was holding one of its meetings. I was there together with my wife, Anne Marie, and one of my earlier PhD students, Hans Strikwerda, now professor at the University of Amsterdam and head of a large research-institute, the Nolan Norton. As Hans and Madelyn conversed, it soon became clear that the research that Madelyn had done in international organizations such as the International Monetary Fund and the World Bank, where she was one of the first female division managers ever, would eminently serve as basis for a practice-rooted dissertation as Hans had made himself before.

Madelyn and I then engaged in conversation and came to an agreement – the beginning of one of my most remarkable and inspiring paths of my career.

I was immediately struck by the enormously precise and clear way of Madelyn's thinking and writing – every word, every sentence well formed and exactly in place, like a mathematical flow with a poetic overtone. Of course, she graduated from one of the most, if not 'the' most prestigious business school in the world, the Wharton Business School in Philadelphia, and one might expect at least some marks of such a great Eden. But there was more, because her very best school, as I later found out, was the school she seems to carry with her even today, her mother and father – and probably in that order. I wished I could repeat the entire dedication she wrote on the first part of her dissertation, but one single sentence may carry the flavour: "...My father talked about being true to myself, but my mother gave me the tools and attitude to find and achieve myself. I owe her...". You immediately sense a woman here – Madelyn – who has learned to do what it takes, not by shouting at barricades, but by simply doing it, perfectly, performing elegantly, like her mother.

Likewise, I, too, gained strong inspiration from women who became the accompaniers and co-practitioners in my learning with Madelyn. First Mary Gergen, who really helped in building structure and by asking questions. Then Tineke Willemsem, who became co-supervisor and helped to finalize the product in good order. Both were academic professors in women's studies, highly sharp and critical, but immensely dedicated, like Madelyn herself. But also my wife, Anne Marie, who, without being a professor in women's studies, acted like one, and made Madelyn, her husband Gerald, and even her piano-playing niece, Ariana, part of our family. They all played a part in the cast of what became a great play.

Madelyn became a role-model herself. Soon after finishing her dissertation, the Taos Institute, under the inspiring guidance of its president, Kenneth Gergen, built a Ph.D. program with my University at Tilburg, to write more dissertations like the one Madelyn had written, that is of highly performing, reflective practitioners, whose tacit knowledge very much deserves the scholarly articulation that can inspire other practitioners and scholars in the same field. The guiding spirit of this program is the one that also underlies the new book of Madelyn, that is the relational constructionism – the idea that meaning and value, or what we cherish as knowledge and the good, is constantly created and maintained in communities of practice. This has always been so. But in a pre-modern or modern world, where communities can live on their own, or where, when they move and communicate, they can do this with objectifying power on others, it does not strike so clearly. But in the current postmodern world, where we constantly deal with other people from many different communities, without the possibility to dominate or to excommunicate when encountering difference, the acknowledgement of the relational character of what we know and what we value has become a virtually inevitable necessity. This has all been articulated and debated at length in many publications of members of the Taos Institute, not the least in those of its president, Kenneth Gergen. Madelyn's new book *Riding the Current*, however, is a perfect illustration of how these experiences and conceptions 'can' and, I dare to say 'should' be translated in participatory practices of learning and development for people who, on average, live longer than ever, and need to stay fresh in knowledge and want to keep their work alive.

Without going back in detail to all the philosophical and epistemological underpinnings, but also clearly without ignoring them, Madelyn has managed to create very practical lessons from these intellectual resources. Her own immense experience in consulting and coaching, in top line management, in running her own business, and in communicating with other scholars and practitioners, has given her a unique basis to do this.

I cannot refrain from thinking now of the preface which Lee Cronbach, who later became president of the American Psychological Association, wrote for his book on Educational Psychology, now about half a century ago. He said that books of this type should be judged on their relevance for the people who need it, their being based on evidence, their doing justice to the complexity of human behaviour, and their clarity, so that people who want to use it can really read and understand it. Dear Madelyn, your book is written in a new area, with new inspirations and other targets, but will definitely also do very well on these ancient criteria. We, including me, owe you a lot. Thanks.

John Rijsman, Ph.D.
Professor of social psychology at the faculty of social sciences
Tilburg University (The Netherlands)

Preface

I was very pleased when Madelyn Blair asked if I would contribute a preface to the present work. Madelyn has been a close friend and stimulating colleague for over 15 years. Here was a lovely opportunity to pay credit to all I have learned from her, and all she has contributed to me, to the Taos Institute, and to the organizational world at large. At the same time, the invitation was daunting. I was overwhelmed with commitments, and daily the email brought with it dozens of additional issues to which I should attend. And this was to say nothing of the accumulating journals in the stacks around my desk, unopened manuscripts to which I should respond, and books sent on to me by various friends and publishers. I was overwhelmed and rudderless. How, then, was I to find a moment to respond to Madelyn's welcoming invitation?

As I began to read through the manuscript, however, the answer struck me between the eyes. Surely I would contribute a Preface, for this book was going to speak exactly to my condition of aimless overload. It is not simply the ever-expanding sea of connections made available through the internet. There is also the explosion of websites, which demonstrate to us that for virtually any topic in which we have an interest, there may be thousands of relevant sites. Mastery is impossible, the accumulation continuous, and motivation retreats. How shall we cope; is it even worth a try? Then on top of this, there is also the burgeoning of new social network facilities – Facebook, Twitter, LinkedIn, and High 5, and on and on – inviting 24/7 communication. We swim in a sea of information, and we all sense the dread of drowning.

It is in this context that I find Madelyn's writing not only refreshing and reassuring, but wonderfully instructive. With compelling clarity she lays out the steps we might follow, not only to generate a tactic for orienting ourselves in this world of information overload, but to keep our interests alive and our knowledge useful. I found especially helpful her emphasis on the way in which our relationships contribute to staying fresh and focused. To some degree we must make personal decisions, but not without being conscious of the communities of practice to which we belong and the particular organizational contexts in which we labor. And within such communities of practice, Madelyn emphasizes the significance of conversation with others. Through conversations with practice partners, she points out, issues become alive for us, their contours take shape, and we begin to direct our information-search and appropriation in ways that are effective. Here I recall the lively breakfast room conversations between Madelyn and my wife, Mary Gergen, during the period in which Madelyn was writing her PhD dissertation. Mary was serving as one of her advisors at the time, and I can now see in these catalytic conversations the concept of the practice partner in vivid color.

   Riding the Current speaks cogently to the condition of our times. We all ride more safely, sanely, and effectively with Madelyn Blair at the helm.

Kenneth J. Gergen

President, The Taos Institute

Riding the Current

Riding the Current: How to Deal With the Daily Deluge of Data

Introduction

This book offers a new way to keep your knowledge fresh through conscious self-guided learning that is grounded in the world of those around you. It is an approach that can be applied directly to work, avocations and passions. The approach is built on several disciplines that recognize that the question 'What do you know?' can't be answered directly; that discovery and creation of new knowledge is done in conversation with others; and that our stories offer a wealth of insight.

A word about the word *fresh*. Staying current implies a perfection that is unachievable. No one I talked with feel they remain current in their fields whether they are completely lax in keeping up or stellar in keeping up. They see their knowledge in relation to the mass of information that is known rather than in relation to what they could know. Yet, they do feel they can keep fresh their knowledge by consciously attending to it in full recognition that knowing it all is not possible. In this book, I will use this wonderful word *fresh*.

This book draws on my experience and the experience of over fifty people interviewed. It combines that knowledge base with theory and exercises to present an approach that is powerful and easy to understand. Regardless of your focus—work, avocation, passion or all three—this book will be useful.

This book will help you discover ways in which your learning can occur outside the classroom and beyond books, journals, blogs, wikis, magazines and podcasts. It will help to illuminate the ways in which we all learn every day—and can learn more, as we become more aware of *how* we learn.

As you explore the exercises and advice of this book, you will experience the critical questions faced by anyone interested in managing her own desire to keep her knowledge fresh and alive. In the process of doing this, you will be exploring the general topic of *knowledge management* at the individual level, sometimes called personal knowledge management. (This book will tend not to use this language, preferring to talk about keeping knowledge fresh and about riding the current.)

Who is your crew on the journey, as you learn how to 'ride the current'? If you are on the staff of an organization, you will see that supervisors, colleagues and team members can become real supporters as you explore and create approaches for keeping your knowledge fresh and alive. My long-term friend, Brenda Hermann, has suggested that supervisors should really think of themselves as accompanying their staff. The concept of "accompanying" offers a freedom that some supervisors may not normally feel, by suggesting that as supervisors they are just journeying with you, the staff, accompanying you in workplace activity.

In some cases, supervisors become active participants in the creation of their staff members' learning plans. After all, supervisors are part of your day-to-day life. While not a requirement, I recommend involving your supervisor in the exercises of this book – when appropriate. In truth, any learning process involves everyone in your world. The level of involvement will depend on your relationship with them.

Those who are struggling to find new ways to become more useful to the work unit (and more employable) will find the participation of a supervisor useful. Those who are established in their careers will find the help of a colleague more useful. (I introduce the term Practice Partner in the book and talk about this new role for the lifelong learner.) If you are interested in remaining fresh in your field, staying up to date in areas relevant to your work, pushing the boundaries of your own understanding in order to grow, or simply pursuing a life of ongoing learning, you will find value in including your colleagues and supervisor as you pursue this approach.

In all cases, the approach is only useful if individuals find it valuable to do the exercises laid out here. Many steps are presented in this book. Not all of them apply to every reader. To help in selecting the most valuable for you, please begin with the short self-administered survey found in Chapter 1. Your results will suggest areas you may wish to target first.

Plan to pursue the steps suggested by your assessment. This will lead you to a clear set of actions that take into account your natural and developed strengths and skills. These actions will lead to achievement of goals that can satisfy both professional and personal desires. The insights you gain and the behaviors you develop will support your future learning. Moreover, for those who choose, you will have a Practice Partner who may continue at your side as your lifelong learning unfolds.

Reasons to Read This Book

People who are striving to be 'world-class' seek out information on what it takes to achieve greatness. Geoff Colvin's book, *Talent Is Overrated: What Really Separates World-Class Performers from Everybody Else,* is one of the more recent in a parade of self-help manuals for the professionally ambitious. Colvin debunks myths of exceptional performance, placing his bets on practice, deep knowledge and perseverance—paths to greatness available to any of us who make the time to pursue them. But maybe striving to be 'world class' isn't your main objective. Maybe it's simply the right season in your life for you to acquire some new skills for staying current in the areas important to you. Perhaps you recognize yourself in one or more of the following examples.

In one of my recent studies, an interviewee told me that once out of school, he found that he used in his work only 10% of what he had learned in school. The rest of the time, he used what he had learned about the organization in order to get things done. He was frustrated after so many years to use so little of his substantive background. Having said this, he realized that his work really required a bit more of him. Clients demand the best solutions. While he could be effective in the organization, he knew he wasn't spending time refreshing his substantive knowledge to assure he brought to the client's problems the best he could manage. In today's world, competition demands more of all of us.

I know young professionals who want to make a difference in the world. It is not a matter of just making a living, but participating in work that improves the world. One young professional determined that she would learn whatever background and skills were necessary for her to do a useful job once she found an organization in whose mission she could believe. Seeking new understanding and skills means on-going learning.

Mid-career professionals often find that they do not have the knowledge it takes to get to the next level. Preparing for advancement involves learning new skills, gaining exposure to new experiences, and in all assuring that the knowledge and understanding being brought to the situation is fresh. I know an aspiring manager who realized that being able to speak to large audiences had become important, and he must add this new skill to his tool kit. For him, the question became how to fit learning this skill into the current activities of a busy career. This aspect—fitting new learning into a busy life—is not restricted to those in professions alone. Just imagine how much carpenters, plumbers and electricians must learn to bring new products to their customers to meet today's more complex needs. While craftspeople learn in different ways from professionals, the technologies they use and how they are applied change all the time.

Retirees often decide to make the end of one career the start of another. The new career may be a volunteer activity, a new business or a shift to focus on a passion. For each, there is the need to refresh the great reservoir of knowledge in order to best leverage a life of experience.

Throughout the stages of work and life, there are people who constantly wish to expand their understanding of the world and the relationships they have within it. Lifelong learners tend to be driven by this goal regardless of their individual work or interest.

As these examples illustrate, there are as many reasons to read this book as there are individuals with goals that require keeping knowledge fresh and alive.

Who Can Use This Book

- Those who wish to become 'world class.'
- Individuals who are already inspired to remain fresh and knowledgeable
- Supervisors, team leaders and managers who sincerely want to help staff to develop in their abilities and careers, or want to enrich the learning environment of their teams.
- Those who wish to advance in their career.
- Parents who wish to find a new way to inspire their children to learn—or themselves.
- Retirees who wish to move toward their passions with greater knowledge and know-how.
- Anyone who is a lifelong learner!

Benefits for Leaders as Well

"Organizations learn only through individuals who learn." - Senge, 1990

I have spent years in the workforce in leadership positions. Knowing that people are at the center of productivity, I have been concerned with developing staff. I have created this book with the needs of those who are responsible for the development of others in mind.

A powerful means to engage individuals is to seek ways in which pursuing their own interests can be aligned with those of the organization. "Seventy-three percent of the U.S. workforce is disengaged, costing the U.S. economy 300 billion dollars a year. These are the people who are not only unhappy at work, but are busy acting out their unhappiness ...[and] actively [undermining]what their engaged coworkers accomplish."[1] The approach presented in this book can be used to assist in re-engaging staff. Some would look at this as only good for business, but in truth, those who are engaged in their work can find more satisfaction in their whole lives. It works both ways.

Everyone desires the opportunity to be employed. Outsourcing, the global economy, and financial pressures have placed additional burdens on people to show value for their contributions to the company. While skills are essential, it is knowledge that is the best demarcation of potential value. Creating an environment where the acquisition of knowledge is supported serves both the individual and the leader.

Today's workers are faced with complex problems that demand deeper understanding before resolution can be obtained. This deeper understanding requires knowledge that is broad, contextual, and fresh. Even teams must be aware of their combined knowledge, if they are to bring the right mix to bear on the problem.

Young people see the world differently. They tend to be more engaged with their friends and colleagues, and desire to have a positive impact on the world from their work.[2] They hope to join an organization where they can be interested in the mission, really understanding it, and see how they contribute. Supervisors of these young people need to realize that keeping them engaged in the workplace includes giving them opportunities for understanding and ongoing learning.

---

[1] Curt Coffman, "Building a Highly Engaged Workforce: How Great Managers Inspire Virtuoso Performance," Gallup Management Journal, 3 June 2002.

[2] Sylvia Ann Hewlett, " How Gen Y & Boomers Will Reshape Your Agenda," Harvard Business Review, July/August 2009.

New technologies are introducing changes in the world at an increasing rate. All of us must learn new skills and concepts, just to survive in this kind of world.[3] To remain at top form (or even reasonable form) demands the same in the workplace. Lifelong learning is no longer an option—it is an essential. Besides, it makes life much more interesting.

In working with people over the years, I have found that everyone struggles with the creation of plans for achieving career goals (called development plans in organizational-speak). I can remember managers reduced to jelly as they attempted to create development plans for their staff. This was usually because the affected people were not invited into the process, let alone encouraged to be the initiator of it. With an approach that can assure individual initiative with clear linkage to business goals and supervisor participation, the most vexing challenges of creating development plans are solved. Developing a plan together creates a plan that is naturally motivating, with accountability built in.

If you are affected by any of these organizational issues, you will find solutions in the approach described in this book.

Develop Your Learning Plan

The real returns of any plan come from building it with care, then working through the steps. An effective plan also requires attention to your relationships—relationships essential to exploring and finding new knowledge and supporting ongoing learning.

---

[3] Pink, D.H. "A Whole New Mind: /Why Right-Brainers Will Rule The Future," Riverhead Trade; Rep Upd edition (March 7, 2006)

This book assumes that the reader is interested in developing a personal approach for remaining fresh. I've structured the book to serve that objective.

The approach begins with a self-assessment to determine the areas where your time can best be spent. The assessment will direct you to the chapters of greatest interest or need for **you**. In the chapters, I introduce a number of concepts, explain what each concept contributes to the approach, and offer examples and activities to help you along. Regardless of your reasons for pursuing the creation of a personal plan to keep your knowledge fresh, you need goals. My approach, starting with the self-assessment, helps in the creation of incremental goals.

Few of us have the luxury to dedicate large amounts of time to learning for its own sake. But in case you choose to study the entire process, I have presented my approach in sequential steps that can be tackled as a thorough course of study.

Lastly, any learning plan involves reprogramming behaviors—something that is best done incrementally, one change at a time. Even if you choose to study the entire process sequentially as it's described in this book, I recommend that you tackle it one chapter at a time, giving yourself interludes between steps to allow for bringing change into your life in stages.

This book is also designed to be a reference over time. Riding the current is never a one-time event—it is a way of living. With experience, a step that felt hard to do the first time will be easier the next time. Moreover, it will reward with greater insights discovered the second, third (and more) times you review each step.

The approach described here is a model of the critical elements for a knowledge plan. It offers direction on using your understanding of the approach to build a plan that will meet your needs and desires. It should give hope to those who feel confused by the issue or the enormity of the task. Take heart: No one really learns alone, or entirely on their own.

> I speak of a learning plan but what I offer is more than a plan—it's an entire approach, developed through extensive experience and research. I will show you how to tailor my approach so it becomes **your** approach, adapted to your own learning style and situation. I'll guide you to start using your customized learning plan to begin riding the current, keeping your knowledge fresh and alive. Finally, I'll show you how revisiting the book and your work in the exercises will reward you with greater insights. Just like Howard Milner learning from his own paper written as a student thirty years earlier, (See chapter 1) you'll become your own teacher, creating for yourself the climate you need to achieve lifelong learning.

About the Language I Choose

All writers make choices of voice, style and tone to best communicate with their readers. I like to use language that is clear, direct and free of jargon. Here's one example: In this book, I use the word *lesson* when referring to that which has been learned. Many people use the word *learnings* and are able to communicate effectively. For myself, I prefer the perfectly fine English word *lesson*.

My approach recognizes and includes the essential roles of other people around the learner. I will introduce you to the concept of the *Accompanier* and the *Practice Partner*. In Chapter 1, I will introduce you to the Accompanier, a term for those who play the role of supervisor, teacher, colleague, or mentor of a learner. Each chapter includes sections designed to help the Accompanier work together with those who have decided to develop a learning approach. Moreover, for those who are tasked with creating development programs for their staff, this approach offers a solid way in which the staff members can participate as partners in this work, serving individual as well as organizational goals. When the individual is self-motivated to pursue creating a plan, the Accompanier can act as a mirror of support.

I will explain the rationale for finding a Practice Partner who will become an ongoing companion in learning. A Practice Partner is a person you can call upon to assist you in your thinking as you move through the approach. Often people choose a colleague in their field, but some of the best are from fields outside one's own. Why this is so will be revealed in Chapter 3.

Lastly, you may also find a fellow seeker who is one who decides to develop his or her own plan while you are developing yours. As both of you do the activities, the conversation is enriched by the mutual experiences — but more about this later.

Finally, a note on my use of personal pronouns: Because English lacks a non-gender-specific singular third-person pronoun that applies to people, I will use both he and she randomly to avoid the gender bias of the traditional masculine singular or the grammatical lapse of the plural pronoun used when the subject is singular.

What You Will Find in This Book

Each chapter is grounded in stories and responses from those interviewed to enliven and provide examples of the material presented. Each chapter offers exercises, some that prepare you for the action steps required and others that direct your actions. At the end of each chapter, I ask you to reflect on what you have learned, and to record both your lessons learned and possible options for action. In this way, you capture your learning and prepare for the next chapter you address — whether it's the next in sequence or not. These sections are clearly marked so that you can use them as reference.

Sidebars in each chapter speak directly to the Accompanier, explaining that role in the context of the chapter, with suggestions for actions to support the seeker of knowledge — you, the primary reader. In this way, I've designed a structure that keeps you focused on the material most useful for you, and also guides the others you invite to support and accompany you.

Chapter 1, Setting Out, is all about deciding to set out on this voyage of discovery. It addresses questions such as: What does keeping knowledge fresh and alive entail? What compels you to continuing learning? This chapter challenges you to take the lead through a decision about your commitment. It also presents a graphic depiction of the various stages that make up my learning approach. (The graphic reappears in subsequent chapters, as I introduce each stage and its required actions.) This chapter introduces the Accompanier, describing the places where the Accompanier's participation is both essential and helpful. Lastly, this chapter offers a self-assessment tool that will help you determine the best place for you to begin your voyage, as you prepare to ride the current.

Chapter 2, Selecting the Vessel, helps you build your boat — the container that keeps you focused, working effectively within a chosen structure. It explores how individuals decide on which subjects to focus, when so much competes for our attention. With a carefully constructed container, setting your objectives and choosing a direction in which to head out becomes much easier and safer, too. With this chapter, you are taking the time to link what it is you think you want or need to do about learning to your own goals and, in some cases, the goals of your organization. Finding these linkages is critical to developing a successful learning approach. Completing the exercises in this chapter will prepare you to ride the current, even as it takes you into uncharted waters. Don't skip it.

Chapter 3, Finding the Right Crew, describes the value of surrounding yourself with people to support your learning. It explores the importance of conversation to learning, and even defines the type of conversation that will energize you again and again. It shows how stories nourish the relationships that keep the crew functioning effectively. It introduces several specific roles for members of the crew, especially the strategy of choosing a Practice Partner. With the right vessel and crew, the journey can begin.

Chapter 4, Stocking Supplies for the Journey, is about using stories and observation as portals to learning. This chapter offers exercises designed to help you gather insights and explore your own strengths and interests from the perspectives of others. This chapter guides you to become a close observer of your environment, in order to steer toward what matters and avoid running aground on the irrelevant. As you ride the current, there will be times you choose to scan a broad horizon, and times you choose to dive deep after a specific treasure. In this chapter I show you how to attain a perspective from which to make these important choices.

Chapter 5, Equipping for the Dive, explores the amazingly diverse ways humans learn. For you to dive deep after fresh knowledge, you must have specialized equipment, tailored to fit—learning techniques matched to your own personality and strengths. We all learn through different means. This chapter reviews different strategies, then presents opportunities to practice specific approaches, to find what works best for you. Further, the chapter offers an optional exercise to explore how new knowledge is created. This mission, if you accept the challenge, will remind you what creative creatures we all are.

 Chapter 6, Deciding to Dive Deep, is about capturing lessons learned from the work so far. With each chapter you've completed, you have been recording lessons learned and possible options for action. Now you are invited to look more closely—to dive deeper. It's scary to dive off the edge of the boat, yet there are gems to be found by exploring the water itself. This chapter helps you to see the potential of stepping out of your safe space and exploring beyond your normal boundaries. Stories of those who have learned to thrive in uncharted water will inspire you to discover the lessons beyond the surface. It will help you discover the riches already contained in your reservoir of knowledge that were invisible from the surface. The chapter then invites you to put your lessons together and integrate them. This can be fun even as it is challenging.

Chapter 7, Taking Charge: Deciding What to Do, leads you through action planning—actually defining your own customized learning approach in such a way that you can revisit it, building your skill at riding the current through iterative rounds of discovery and practice. You decide the format for the plan, and this chapter helps you to complete it. Finish the exercises in this chapter and I doubt you'll ever again feel adrift in an ocean of too much information.

 Chapter 8, Final Words, encourages you to use the treasures you've found on this voyage. You'll discover that the spiral patterns found everywhere in nature apply to riding the current as well, as you review the work you've done in Chapters 1 through 7. Chapter 8 encourages you to continuously dip into the swirl of new knowledge to gather what you need, leading to more fresh knowledge and enlivened work as you ride the current. This chapter offers some final words to the leader in all of us.

Following the eight chapters you will find three annexes offer helpful hints for pursuing fresh knowledge at various stages of the approach. They include: Conducting the Interviews, On Creating the Plan and Writing Your Story. We are all drawn to what we see clearly, so, the last Annex presents ways in which you can take your plan and put the end point into focus. It's fun to do and makes a real difference in the energy you will have for making the plan part of your day-to-day life.

Riding the Current, Fresh and Alive

As I pondered the words those I interviewed gave to me, I was truly struck by the words *fresh* and *alive*. They became such a marker for so many things in my life. Fresh water poured into a glass has an aliveness that even drinking from a bottle of spring water doesn't. It's as if the pouring of the water adds life to it just from the movement. Anyone who has drunk from a flowing mountain stream knows that nothing else is quite as satisfying — lips surrounded by cold, racing water. The current of the water feels active 'all the way down.' Fresh bread from the oven is like nothing else. It satisfies at so many levels. The fragrance, the crunch of the crust and the softness of the interior — each characteristic adds to the experience. Silk flowers are beautiful, but they can never substitute for the vibrancy that spills out of live flowers. If, like me, you like your water fresh and cold, bread fragrant from the oven, or your flowers perky with life, you'll find keeping your knowledge fresh equally satisfying. This book is for you.

Knowledge Management (KM) at the Unit of One (for those who are interested in KM)

"It seems obvious, but it is not often said that knowledge management works best when knowledge workers take the initiative and responsibility for what they know, don't know and need to know." - Steve Barth, "The Power of One," KM Magazine, December 2000

Many people have been working on helping individuals think in terms of knowledge management for themselves. They have called it Personal Knowledge Management (PKM).

This book presents a new approach to this topic, one that is more effective because it is built around the principles of adult learning and successful knowledge sharing techniques. It brings social construction to the conversation—the collaborative processes essential for the construction of reason, knowledge, and human value. The approach models insights from the experiences of these various principles and techniques.

Where does this fit into an organization and its knowledge management strategy? Knowledge Management (KM) has many definitions and variations. However, all of the definitions offer three elements: (1) providing access to knowledge, (2) creating an environment that encourages the sharing of knowledge, and (3) fostering a desire to learn.

Organizations work hard to provide data bases, portals, knowledge assets (a fancy word for a data base that contains nuggets of the wisdom learned by others as they have done their work), communities of practice, and other strategies to help the organization find ways to remember and access what the organization has learned.

Organizations have had less success in creating environments that encourage the sharing of knowledge. The clear exception is communities of practice (communities of *passion* is another name) that have been encouraged and often given resources to help communities enhance their effectiveness. Outside of communities, managers have found it harder to change the behaviors of people who still believe that knowledge hoarded is power. Knowledge lives within communities, and has its greatest effect in communities. This shift in understanding where the real power lies—from hoarding to sharing—is beginning to be seen. However, within communities of passion, people have already decided to share their knowledge because they trust that others will do the same. They have learned that in conversation, knowledge grows beyond the sum of the individual parts.

Building a desire to learn is more difficult. I know that when I teach, my task goes well beyond knowledge transfer (from my head to theirs) to creating a desire in participants to both pull it from me (to assure that they are getting what they need) and to rediscover what they already know. Sometimes, they create new understanding in conversation among participants as they explore the new knowledge in relation to their work setting. My principle job is to provide the opportunity for them to learn. Learning becomes their primary task. In the classroom where the focus is on learning, the participants themselves are still the ones responsible for learning. Consider how much more difficult it is to generate staff responsibility for continuous learning without the structure of the classroom. In the end, organizations don't learn, people learn. Organizations don't act; the people within them act.

Thus, there are always two levels of responsibility in KM—the organization has to do its part, and people must do their part. Organizations need to have practices in place that encourage the sharing of knowledge. The organization must support managers

19

and supervisors who know how to engage individuals in their work. This last point is essential. Real KM only happens when the people involved get fully engaged.

The approach presented in this book requires engagement. It is designed to give individuals insight into how they can enhance their own knowledge to aid them in achieving their goals, while serving in the KM activities of the organization to aid in achieving the organization's goals. The approach also addresses how supervisors, team leaders and managers can become more useful partners in helping staff ride the current of knowledge.

Riding The Current

Setting Out

"Hardened opinions will turn you stale quicker than anything else."-Daniel Dixon, writer, former executive, octogenarian

I am curious. At least so I am told. It took me some time to learn what was really meant by those three words. Was I curious because I asked a lot of questions? I did ask questions. Was I curious because I opened doors to rooms that I had never entered before? I was known to do that. Was I curious because I researched a subject far beyond the original question? Well I did that too.

Through years of reflection I have developed an understanding of myself and my learning techniques that went beyond the word curious. I realized I listened in meetings with intensity, with an insatiable thirst to understand. I find myself describing one subject by referencing an entirely different area, and I gain a new perspective. For example, I might compare staff development to pruning, a common technique used in gardening. Boy, would that start a conversation! I draw from my love of gardening and infuse it into my work with organizations, cross pollinating my knowledge base.

I learn at every opportunity. I heard John Seely Brown, the former head of the Xerox PARC labs make the statement, "Innovation occurs in the white spaces between disciplines." As I sat in the audience, never having met him before that day, he touched me, changed me, and my whole way of thinking shifted. I now love to live in the white spaces between disciplines. It is an exciting place to be. There are unexpected learning opportunities popping up constantly.

In the white spaces – as I thought about those words, my mind conjured images of myself as a college student. I was studying English by reading mathematics. It was as if I needed to find another perspective before I could fully understand or learn or know.

As stories will do, listeners are transported to a new place. I sat at a table with my team. We needed to compose an important communiqué about an upcoming change in the organization. My mind conjured up a memory of a friend who didn't keep his word. How did I feel? I told the story. The story served to create a different perspective. The communiqué almost composed itself. The solution was so clear. Stepping from the known to an open space allows me to find unexpected answers drawn from other situations—existing knowledge with a new perspective.

I continued to seek a deeper understanding of how curiosity had enriched my life. What Seely Brown meant by the white spaces. How I can walk into a clearing and see the forest. How everyday I sail beyond the horizon to find a new shore.

You will never again feel as if you are trying to drink from a fire hose, drowning in a deluge of information. *Riding the Current* is the codifying of my techniques that I have developed over the years that enable me to keep my knowledge fresh and alive - that continuously stimulate my curiosity. I wrote this book to share not only my techniques but my insights and methods that can be customized into a learning approach of your very own.

'Just in Time' Knowledge

No one is able to fully answer the question, "What do you know?" We ask it of each other all the time, yet a direct question about what you know is impossible to answer.

How many times have I stumbled in an attempt to respond comprehensively to a simple question about what I do! Ask me about what I know, and I find it utterly impossible to respond. My mind simply shuts down as if on overload. Besides, so much of what we know can't be expressed in words. How do you tell a person all of your knowledge about riding a bicycle? How do you tell someone how a beef roast smells at just the right moment of doneness? How do you articulate the feeling you get when you see a group coalescing into a real team? Yet any of this knowledge is available to us at the right moment, if we know how to reach for it. We access and expand our knowledge through conversation, through stories, and through playing in the white space between disciplines—and this book will show you how.

I discovered the difficulty of 'knowing what I know' from my own experience. Ask me a general question, and I have so much from which to select that my thought process seems to stop, wanting to know which path it should take. Ask me a specific question, however, and the answer is right there—even at times when I didn't know I knew the answer until I spoke. It's as if it were 'just in time' knowledge, created on the spot. The question drew it from me like a pump draws water from a well. No wonder conversing with friends clarifies thinking. Clearly, we all know things we didn't know we knew until we are asked.

In response to a direct question, I might first look within my discipline. Ask me about a management issue, and I first consider the management theory I know. When the answers I find there are not sufficient, I look for familiar patterns in other disciplines. Suddenly, I realize that the situation looks like the time I tried to make beef stew with too much water or too little salt to bring out the flavor. So, what is the 'water' in the original issue? Is 'salt' needed? If I find the 'water' or the 'salt,' I usually find the answer.

Then there are those times when a story leaps to mind in response to a question. How fortuitous these times are. The stories of my life are part of my very self and always there for me to recall. Stories by their nature contain within them more than the facts—they carry meaning, which is drawn from the story by the listener. When you tell yourself one of your very own stories, don't be surprised if you discover a new insight from it yourself. As you reflect on a particular day and the information you have gathered throughout it, the stories you spin about that day help you find the meaning and gain insights. Stories offer us a safe place to play with our knowledge.

Seely Brown was right. Innovation occurs in the white spaces between disciplines. Conversation enhances our ability to draw from our reservoir of knowledge; from different disciplines we can gain enormous insights; and story opens the field of possibilities. With these thoughts in mind, I conceived this book.

Why Write "Riding the Current"

"I can't imagine – not ever – not being curious. Boredom plays a role in integrating information and learning to entertain the self."- Kat Pearl, teacher

Throughout my career I have been aware of the importance of having the right information to do the job at hand. Perhaps it came from my years in institutional analysis; perhaps it came from working with so many executives as they struggled to define what information they needed for their decisions; perhaps it came from years of working with information technology as it slowly became the dreamed-of technology that we enjoy today, or perhaps it came from my mother.

I arrived at the World Bank a fresh MBA graduate from Wharton, plus two years at IBM with all the latest information on management and technology. When I left the World Bank ten years later, I realized that I had learned very little new about management or technology or anything other than how to make things happen at the Bank. I was successful in my work at the Bank. I understood my short-term goals and achieved them. I figured out how to motivate staff. But I didn't have a handle on current events, a major aspect of the Bank's larger mission, or anything that was essential to the long-term goals of my work at the Bank. I was astounded at myself. Why hadn't I gone to conferences? Why had I not read? Here I was a person basically curious about everything, yet ignoring so many important areas of life. In those 10 years, I had not spent one minute developing myself or even keeping current in management or technology.

The good news was that I knew how to create staff development plans. I had developed plans based on business needs and related the competencies of each staff member. To serve them, I developed projects that would allow a staff member to learn about the work by teaming up with another who already knew it. I found ways for staff to take courses if we couldn't find in-house classes, and I would justify it in relation to the work plan. As a result, I ended up with some remarkably educated staff who continued to apply their knowledge, advancing themselves to higher levels of work. I had gotten them to tap into their own creative space. They were fantastically productive and morale was so high, it was off the charts. They loved it, and so did I. I could do this for my staff, but neglected to do it for myself. So, what was the problem with me?

If I could help others find their creative spirit, increase their desire to learn, explore options that seemed unfamiliar, and stay the course, I surely must know more than I thought. This more was also something that I was not practicing for myself. It was then that I remembered my mother.

My mother is a great cook. Everyone wants to eat at her table. When at the age of 76, she took a cooking class, I asked her why. Her response was simple, direct, and one I had heard many times growing up. "You can always learn, Madelyn." Even when pressed with day-to-day duties, my mother never lost her curiosity, her ability to see what was happening around her and learn from it. Why had I forgotten this lesson of the value of learning just because I had been busy with my work at the Bank? I had to examine my own self to learn the lessons about learning. When I did, I created for myself something that has worked ever since. I have been able to allow my curiosity to blossom once again. I keep a constant eye out for what is happening around and within me so that I am on a constant upward learning curve. I articulate long-term goals in ways they remain visible to me so that the short-term doesn't obscure them. I have found the companions who act as sources and sounding boards so that my understanding is tested, enhanced, and embellished.

Through this self-reflection and purposeful action, I have seen amazing results. Clients are often telling me how I bring them the latest information, how I see nuances in issues that have escaped their attention, how I come up with solutions that work. I knew I had to share this with others. I had to convey that it is possible even when you are working long hours under pressure. I had to define the steps, the behaviors, the secrets of how I had done it and how anyone can ride the current and keep their knowledge fresh and alive.

Over the years, I had begun coaching line managers. Quickly I learned that my experience was not unique. There were few line managers who had time to keep their knowledge up to date. But the more I worked with clients, the more I realized there were other problems.

First, the technical staff members were not remaining current either. They spent time learning how to get things done in their organizations rather than getting the latest in their areas of 'expertise.' Then I began to encounter the individual who really wanted to keep his knowledge up to date but was frustrated because he could get no support from management—no budget for travel, no budget for training, no time for developmental assignments, nothing. Management considered them mid-career professionals who knew what they needed to know. Why should the organization invest further in them?

At the same time, line managers were being asked to create staff development plans. If I could find one manager who knew how to do this, I would do cartwheels. Normally, managers tended to just list in-house courses for each staff member and feel they had done their duty. I knew better than that.

For the last twenty years, the already-rapid pace of change has only quickened. Technology continues to offer new options. New products, approaches, ideas are coming at an increasing rate. And then the Internet became reality, and information is available as it has never been before. At first, the challenge was finding information. Does anyone remember the world before Google? Today, the flood of available information is impossible to manage. With blogs, collaborative spaces, list serves, wikis, Skype, and other tools that make it possible to fill every moment of the day accessing information, it feels like drinking from a fire hose. We are more connected, yet feel a sense of loss as we know so much is passing us by.

Problems faced by organizations are complex in nature. Knowledge to solve them must be both deep and broad. How do people prepare themselves for such a task?

Today's linked economy is putting enormous pressure on companies to face successfully more and more competition. Having staff with an interest in learning is an essential investment for the organization as well as for the individual. Theorists used to talk about *lifelong learning*. Today, it is no longer a theory. It is life for those who want to survive, let alone thrive. It's the survival kit for any manager who wants to come out of this economic downturn with his or her flag flying high.

Innovation has been one of the engines of our economy, but innovation requires knowledge—deep knowledge aligned with good creative thinking. Yes, creative thinking is essential, but it is not sufficient. Knowledge is a part of the equation.

As a management consultant I had to be aware of these forces and know the latest insights on how to help organizations contend with the challenges of a global economy and the deep need to innovate. Where was my level of knowledge? How current was it really? I had to do something about it. If I could do it for my staff, I knew I could do it for myself. I just needed the will to do it.

But drawing from history alone does not reflect the flows of information today. I wanted to be sure that my insights were reflective of how others have dealt with similar kinds of challenges in their own fields, and I wanted to learn from them in context. I had to hear stories, and they had to be current ones. I decided to interview people.

Going after interviews turned out to be the perfect way to bring fresh insights and knowledge to the exploration of how to keep current. I purposely chose people ranging from those still in school to those who had already led rich lives. Their ages spanned 65 years, ages 17 to 82 to be exact. I purposely chose people from many different fields—economist, artist, carpenter to name a few. This broad spectrum of people brought deep riches to the topic and diverse stories.

While I anticipated some differences, I didn't expect to discover an immediate common thread across all of them. When asked how they kept themselves current, they all said in one form or another that it was not possible any more to remain current. They spoke of wanting to remain fresh.

'Staying current' had to be redefined as remaining in the flow of new information, rather than trying to gather all information in a comprehensive way. The question became how to stay in the flow of things to keep fresh. Suddenly, I was in a new place. I could almost see myself in a small boat riding the current of a river. The current was swift so that I was moving along at quite a clip. The landscape on either side passed by me, my eyes dwelling on one feature and then another. The landscape was open in some places and in other places, deeply lush. I wanted to explore what looked like a building among the trees. As I imagined steering the boat over to the bank, I suddenly realized that what these people were telling me was that they allow the **current** to keep them aware of new knowledge, and they steer toward specifics only when necessary. They had found a way to create a boat and then to direct it. Perhaps this book could help others discover ways to build and direct their boats as well.

Interviews Produce Gems: Three Examples

Gathering stories from the interviews was the start of the process. As often happens when strong people are given open-ended questions, there is an additional bonus. Unexpected gems sparkle through. Let me demonstrate by talking about three of my interview subjects.

Have you ever heard of someone who is always on the leading edge yet never reads the literature? Bob Sadler, head of Sadler Consulting, is said to be one of the leading management consultants in the country. As I talked with him, it was clear that he understood his subject. But when he said that he never read anything but good fiction, you could have knocked me over with a feather. I asked, "You never read any of the management literature?" He said that there were other sources of knowledge that were just as effective. "I have a large network of people with whom I stay in contact. They tell me what they are doing and what they are reading and trying with their clients. I learn about all the latest ideas. And because I am in conversation, I can ask questions to understand. I enter those conversations with an open mind, and I may use the ideas in my own way. Because of my extensive work with my clients, I am well aware of the broad, global trends, which I am able to share with [those who tell me what they have been reading]. It's fair to both sides of the conversation."

Developing a great network of colleagues takes time. Bob has an advantage in that he has been doing what he does for many years. He never seems to pass up an opportunity to meet others, a strategy that anyone can follow. Conversations in the context of subjects that interest us can provide vast amounts of new knowledge. What a boon to those of us with reading piles that are measured in feet. Could it be that strategic conversations can

provide the same (and maybe more) fresh knowledge than reading that looming stack?

Do you ever feel you are going to lose your mind if you got even one more piece of information? What if your job was to gather more and more? Claudia L'Amoreaux is a learning coach and expert in Second Life. The Claudia I knew was quiet and contemplative. She has amazingly deep, complex thoughts yet relates to others gently. I was in for a wonderful surprise when I interviewed her. I knew that she worked with computers, but they didn't seem to be the center of her life. I was stunned to learn that she receives and must process hundreds of emails a day. Her work requires a flow of information and knowledge that very much depends on links and electronic papers. People send her items they feel would be of interest to her, and she sends them similar material.

During our interview she spoke eloquently of making certain that she retains some open time during the day to allow this vast content to be integrated into her thinking. Then I recognized the quiet, contemplative Claudia I had known. Her words gave me a vision of someone barraged by papers, walking through a door into a completely open space with just a large chair waiting for her. As she sits down and closes her eyes, the papers begin to fly around and slowly drift into neat piles, where they momentarily shimmer and then — pop — disappear. When she leaves with a smile, the space is again empty except for the chair.

Claudia showed me that although we live in a great torrent of information, rich with sources of knowledge, we can learn to handle it without losing our minds. We just need to give ourselves a bit of quiet time — unburdened by agendas, time that feels more like 'play' than 'work.' I left my conversation with Claudia pondering the question, how important is 'play' time to taking in the lessons of the day? Does play, like stories, open up white space?

Do you always see what you are looking at? Are you always aware of the sounds around you? When I interviewed Howard Milner, I began to see the shift in awareness that is possible when you work at seeing what is before you and listening to the sounds around you. Milner is a well-known former opera singer who now dedicates his life to coaching people to find their voice.

The evening I arrived for the interview, I was immediately struck by the fact that the air was filled with the songs of birds. The interview was being held in his back yard. I record my interviews, and I found it equally exciting to hear the birds in the background behind Milner's words. It was almost as if I was being taught to hear again, to listen carefully to what was in my environment. As I listened to Milner speak, I heard a similar refrain. He learns by listening carefully, by observing his students, by constantly watching his own actions and reactions to his students and their work—carefully.

"Innovation in my own practice, my own discipline, is the search for excellence...I think, I do tai chi, and I do extreme mountain biking. I try to bring together those three diverse, and incredibly similar, pursuits. As I do that, I am shown and driven to new insights. Innovation is the ability to have insight and then deliver it," says Howard Milner who has discovered how the insights in one discipline come from interaction with other disciplines.

The implications of reflection didn't hit home until Milner told an anecdote that showed me another facet of his learning strategy. Early in his career, he wrote a paper while at school. His teacher admired the work greatly and told him that it would take thirty years to understand it. Milner said that now, thirty years later, he is indeed beginning to understand what he had written. He is using his current work, interpreted with insights from other disciplines, to bring freshness to the ideas he had written down thirty years earlier. What a strange reverse of what we think of as learning. This was living proof that learning and gaining perspective can be turned up side down. He was taking lessons from his own, younger self. His story prompted me to wonder—are we always willing to seek out such unusual perspectives?

Interviews with people like Bob Sadler, Claudia L'Amoreaux, and Howard Milner brought me to an exploration that continues throughout this book. People who recognize that knowledge must be refreshed constantly with new information, new insights and new ideas use surprisingly different techniques for doing so. With solid foundations in their topics, they still remain open, allowing new information to seep in, new insights to bloom, new perspectives to be had.

But let's get back to the subject of keeping your knowledge fresh. When asked about keeping their knowledge current, there was not one who was interviewed who said they **could** keep current. They are focusing on being aware of what is happening. Then, when it is needed, they know exactly when to dive deep into the knowledge.

Throughout this book, you will learn more about each of these individuals, and meet many others who were interviewed. You will find people from fields as disparate as economics and carpentry, acting and scientific research, music and civil service. Their ages span a total of sixty-five years—from high school students to octogenarians. I hope there will be some among them who seem familiar to you. Their stories and comments will provide examples, offer models, inspire and generally give life to the ideas presented here. I'll introduce them to you as they appear and will sometimes add insights about them. By the end of the book, you will have gained insights into some seemingly ordinary people who have found extraordinary ways to live their lives riding the current.

As you read, imagine yourself in conversation with them. Let them join you on your quest as you steer into fresh currents.

Things to Consider as You Take Control of Your Learning

My intent is to convince you to make the decision to begin consciously creating your own approach to learning as you pursue your quest. This shouldn't be a difficult decision for you to reach. After all, you are constantly learning anyway—it's part of your human nature. Learning is an organic process of growth, through processes of adaptation and reproduction. Like every natural process, learning has its growth spurts and its times of apparent quietude. We grow by moving toward or away from stimuli, learning something new from each iteration of stimulus and response. Even in the business world, stripped as it is of most overt references to natural processes, it proves true that learning and the creation of new knowledge take place organically.

So—if it's already a given that you will always be learning, why does deciding to take control of the process matter? It matters because you can make your learning much more effective if you follow an approach tailored to your own personality and life situation.

In upcoming chapters I'll present information drawn from the latest research into learning theory. I'll give you many opportunities to observe others' learning approaches, drawing on my past experience and people I interviewed for this book. I'll offer a number of techniques for integrating lessons learned, from which you can choose those likely to work best for you, whatever your individual learning style. And I'll show you that you don't need to set sail alone, without a structure to keep you afloat. When you enter the sea of new knowledge to be mastered, you'll go with

a supportive craft and crew. You'll be riding the current, keeping your knowledge constantly fresh and alive. But first you must decide to make that your goal. You must commit to the quest.

Practice Partners

I also have a network of friends and colleagues with whom I regularly chat. There are two kinds of colleagues, however. The first are those who think together with me. They ask me questions, offer ideas, probe my rationale, and in all ways encourage my thinking. We often reverse these roles at other times with me asking the questions. I call them my *Practice Partners*. In this book, I'll be talking more about Practice Partners a bit later. These are the people I go back to again and again. They play a major role in helping me keep my knowledge current, fresh, and on the edge. These are like travelers who are curious about where I am going.

Remember that learning doesn't have to be lonely. For years we have been taught that we learn through reading books, going to class, working on our assignments, taking tests. All of these activities have appeared to be done alone. Okay, being in a classroom means being with other people, but when the lecturer talks for fifty minutes, most of the 'learning' is going on in our heads—alone. This gives the impression that all the effort is on our part. Textbooks present the facts or opinions; it is our job to remember them. Lecturers present the truth for us to absorb and master. The assignments are lonely tasks that are as much practices of self-discipline as of learning. And tests are there to assure that we can perform—alone. No wonder we finish school with the feeling that learning is a lonely, independent action, and that it is all up to us to learn by ourselves.

Learning by ourselves? Nothing could be further from the truth. We learn through relating to our world and, especially, in relating to others. We are constantly interacting with what is

37

new, relating it to what we already know.

Remember that knowing is not the same as learning. *Knowledge* is information that can be used to make a decision or take an action. Knowledge capture and dissemination can't remain in the totally logical and rational place where it has traditionally resided—static collections like databases and libraries. It has to serve the mission, but it has to do so by means that help people access knowledge when it is needed and in such a manner that they can learn from it. When we **really** learn, we are able to use the knowledge we've gained either immediately or at any future moment.

Memorizing is not learning. If you don't believe that, think of the first story problem you had to do in math. How was it different from previous math exercises? It had context. You had memorized the multiplication tables, but what were you supposed to multiply with what, and why? Memorizing the multiplication tables was necessary, but it was not sufficient to make them useful. We have to relate the multiplication tables to what we know about the world in which the problem appears. Only then can we solve the problem.

Knowledge has to relate to some context, or it can't be learned. Knowledge without context holds little value. Knowledge and learning are linked. That is why this book focuses on learning as much as on keeping your knowledge current. So, let's take a closer look at *learning*.

Learning is Relational

To learn something, we need to be able to place it into our world, our lives. Learning is done in relationship with other people and ideas. It is done in relation to what we already know – what I call our foundational knowledge. It is done in relation to the context.

Let's begin with relating with other people and ideas. We need the interaction of ideas with our own thinking to create new possibilities. The interaction may include conversation with others or the silent conversation with an author. Marsha Scorza, a licensed professional elementary school counselor, who excels in inviting possibilities within conversations herself, said, "In the course in miracles[4] group, I learn a great deal because of the conversation. The group is made up of people with similar perspectives but new information and an expansive frame of reference, where the discussion is full of lots of possibilities. We share experiences, expand on concepts. I can ask questions and all give their 'take' in responding."

To illuminate the **relational** nature of learning, let's consider a simple example of a crew aboard a ship. Observe how the best of this group's nature serves the needs of one individual— you, the ship's captain.

Your mission is to seek out new knowledge, treasures found somewhere out in a vast sea. You can gather more if you have the right ship, the right crew and equipment, and the approximate coordinates of the treasure.

As captain of the "Knowledge Seeker," you...

- Make sure you have the coordinates, have estimated your travel time, and laid in sufficient supplies. You relate your plans for the journey to the context in which it will take place—time and space.

---

[4] A Course in Miracles is a self-study metaphysical thought system offered through the Foundation for Inner Peace.

- Constantly keep your eyes open to the status of the weather and waves. You watch the compass to maintain a steady course. You listen to the crew to see how they interpret what is going on. You relate to your context—the environment you are passing through.

- Take time to chat over coffee in the galley about the events of the day, the catch, the results of this day's search (for treasure or new knowledge). In conversation, you consider what these finds mean to what you already know. Ideas start to settle into place, connecting the new to the known. You relate to the people journeying with you—your crew.

- At the end of the day, decide what the strategy for tomorrow should be—whether to dive deep beneath the surface, ride the current, seek another current's direction, or return to shore. You relate your plans for the next step to what you already know—what has taken place today.

Communities of Practice

American business, in its search for capturing knowledge, has created databases, portals, and other 'static collections' so that the organization might **remember** what it knows. Watching enormous amounts of information become accessible was exciting. But like remembering the multiplication tables, these rational, logical processes don't support the full range of individual learning. **Knowing the information** has to be brought together with **knowing what it means** in the context of specific situations.

Communities of Practice form when people who have common interests interact. The term refers to groups where people passionate about a topic share their knowledge with one another. They create venues to share information in context, where questions can be posed to assure that both the knowledge and the context are better understood, and where conversation allows listeners to expand the understanding to their own situations.

In these communities, real learning begins to happen so that remembered information becomes **useable**. This kind of interaction doesn't require the formality of a Community of Practice. A colleague, team member or friend can provide the interaction necessary for learning. Notice that we are back to the relational quality of learning.

Now that you've boarded the 'Knowledge Seeker,' look around — you'll visit this place again. In upcoming chapters, you'll find I often return to this ship metaphor when I discuss riding the current. It's a handy way to give form to concepts.

Have you ever left a class feeling that you had learned nothing new, yet it was a valuable experience? Learning knowledge also includes relating the new into what we already know. Bob Sadler of Sadler Consulting spoke of some 'magic hours' he spent in workshops. "I was learning about facilitation and collaboration back in the 1970s with Interaction Associates. I learned how to manage large-scale meetings; how to record them. It was experiential with lots of simulated events. It clarified some things I had done by instinct. It codified what I know to be right from trial and error. But here it was given a framework. I already had the experience. They brought a rigor to it with formal concepts…I had all the puzzle pieces but hadn't put them together. [This training] boosted my confidence." Having a solid framework into which knowledge can be placed reinforces our learning and our retention.

Let's consider how context adds to our learning. Let me give an example. I could never understand why the artists of the Southwest tended to use such bright colors — wild pink, brilliant turquoise. They looked garish to my East Coast eyes. I've created many pieces of art, and there seemed no reason to use such strong colors. Then I moved to Colorado. The sun nearly blinded me, and the colors of my palette appeared washed out and pale.

Suddenly, I saw the context of the bright colors. I understood at a new level. Now, I knew how to use those colors in my own work. I just needed the context to understand.

Create the Right Environment

The best way to have good ideas is to have lots of ideas and throw away the bad ones. Linus Pauling (1901-1994)

Learning is often fed by our curiosity, especially when the environment encourages learning. Consider a one-year-old child who, having just learned to walk, is exploring her world for the first time up on two feet. In a safe environment, the child's curiosity grows until she has explored everything within sight — learning some remarkable lessons along the way. Even mistakes become learning opportunities when the environment is supportive. Exploring eyes and fingers take it all in. Every avenue open to the child becomes an opportunity to learn and a reason to become even more curious. Curiosity moves from topic to topic. It delights in diversity and adapts to new possibilities. Curiosity works in the most illogical ways and stimulates us to seek out more understanding. Have you ever wished your team could explore every aspect of a challenge before selecting the solution?

'We learn from our mistakes' is an oft-quoted truism, yet rarely do we actually encourage mistakes in order to find new lessons. Raymond Douherty had this opportunity. "I suppose a time [I learned best had] more to do with freedom and desperation. I had a suicide attempt, and one of my ex-wives saved me. I came out of the hospital, and I was offered to go to a day center where they had a carpentry project. There I used to make bowls and what not, and then I'd work at home at my own flat. It was all about keeping myself busy. But I learned so much in that time…I tested wood to the limits and used different types of wood. I tried different oils and polishes, paints, whatever. And I'd glue wood together into blocks and make bowls. I'd test them all the time. I

had no fear." Raymond Douherty today is a master carpenter in London. A learning environment must allow for mistakes.

Learning (when the environment is encouraging) has the uncanny ability to produce unexpected and unintended lessons. Think of a time when you sat in a lecture, and an insight came that had nothing to do with what the presenter was saying. A friend of mine who taught at university tells the wonderful story of the time when she assured her students that everything she was going to talk about was in a set of notes she was distributing to them. When one student continued to write as she talked, she reminded him that the notes were coming, and he didn't have to write. His response surprised her and changed her entire perspective. He said, "I'm not taking notes on what you are saying. I'm taking notes on the ideas that I think of as you are talking." Discovering something totally unexpected is one of the delights of being open to learning.

Learning needs the right environment to thrive — an encouraging environment that takes into account human relationships. The toddler's curiosity was encouraged by supportive caretakers, who made sure the environment was safe. The woodworker's experiments in materials and techniques were supported by the staff of the day center he attended, who created a "no fear" atmosphere. The student who took notes on his own ideas, rather than the teacher's, was in a relationship with that teacher, even before the teacher became aware of it.

Whether the learning environment is loose (like the toddler's) or highly structured (like the woodworker's or the student's), it must follow the needs of conversation. It must accommodate emotion and feelings, so necessary for reflection and mistakes. It must allow for new possibilities and curiosity. It must welcome unpredictability.

As these examples demonstrate, learning demands relationships with other people and ideas. It demands a supportive environment where conversation and curiosity can lead to unexpected results, where each new lesson builds on existing knowledge.

Have you ever had a boss who makes it clear he wants to hear only comments that support his position? These kinds of bosses shut down their staff and eventually isolate themselves from reality. Isolation is the opposite of an open learning environment. If you have had such a boss, did you find yourself behaving this way, too? It can be catching. Consider how outcomes might have changed if the organization (and you) understood the full impact of isolating behaviors through shutting down contributions and possibilities.

Open Doors

When I began my work at the World Bank, I observed a division chief who was always busy. His door was open, but his manner was always rushed, distracted. People went to see him only when the situation was critical. It took years to discover that this was a ruse. He just didn't want to be disturbed with other people's problems, and he wasn't. But neither was his unit able to accomplish its mission, and in the next reorganization, it was disbanded.

When I became a division chief, I managed a large unit that served thousands of end users of recently introduced information technology. It had a diverse set of objectives, and there was enormous demand for support. Suddenly I was a busy person. But when staff asked for time with me, I decided that I could not hide behind the excuse of busy-ness. I would give staff my full attention. To make this possible, I asked that they get to the point directly and come in with a recommended action to the issue. I listened to both and then in conversation helped resolve the issue. My unit always achieved objectives, always stayed in budget, and had high morale. It exists to this day more than twenty years later after five reorganizations.

Creating the right environment for conversation can have unexpected and useful results.

In the story "Open Doors," two managers created different environments around themselves. The division chief successfully shielded himself from distractions. I successfully created a vibrant staff while protecting my time. So, what can you do to give yourself the room, the time, the protection to meet your knowledge needs?

If you are saying that you are not a manager and thus can't control this, think again. In the story, the actions that the division chief took were about looking busy all the time. The actions I took were about setting a tone for interaction with others that helped keep the conversation focused and productive. Anyone can learn these simple strategies.

This ability to create the environment should never be dismissed as impossible or of marginal value. Did you know that the Inupiaq of the far north where wood is extremely rare, built houses using whale bones for flooring to insulate from the permanent cold of the ground? It took years to slowly replace the bone with drift wood, the only wood that was available. Creating the desired environment is challenging, but not impossible.

The Context of This Journey

Early organizational knowledge-gathering strategies emphasized formalized and technology-based solutions, and worked at the organizational level. Moving knowledge capture to the individual level must emphasize relational approaches.

The context is better understood where conversation allows listeners to expand the understanding to their own situations. In these communities, real learning begins to happen so that

45

remembered information becomes **useable**. This kind of interaction doesn't require the formality of a Community of Practice. A colleague, team member or friend can provide the interaction necessary for learning. Notice that we are back to the relational quality of learning.

Take the example of writing up 'lessons learned' after a project. (*Lessons learned* is a common phrase that refers to the insights gained through performing or executing a task or activity or project. It helps the participants in the activity as well as the organization by recognizing that everyone at every level has valuable insights.) A traditional knowledge-gathering approach asks the project team to write the 'lesson learned' into the space provided. Individuals are admonished to keep it short so that others will take the time to read it. In the end, the lessons are reduced to something so uninteresting that there is little or nothing of value left. Even those who choose to read them become dissatisfied because their curiosity about context—how the lesson relates to their situation and previous experience—is not satisfied. The reader can't even ask the question. (Newer technologies have recognized this limitation, and allow for telling the story around the lesson as well as contact points to ask questions.)

Context is essential. Learning doesn't occur outside of the context of its application.[5] The traditional knowledge-gathering approach seems efficient, but in my experience, a relational approach is *effective*.

- The very first step is to decide to begin the quest for knowledge. (Chapter 1: Setting out.)

---

[5] "Situated Learning and the Culture of Learning" by John Seely Brown, Allan Collins, and Paul Duguid. www.sociallifeofinformation.com/situated_learning.htm, Accessed August 2006.

- Having made that decision, you must determine the objectives or goals that you are wishing to achieve, i.e., create the right container. (Chapter 2: Designing the Vessel.)

- Recruit your crew, establish how you will work together ('right of way' rules). Create the right climate, using conversation and story to develop shared context/ understanding. Doing the work itself should be influenced and guided by looking at a high proportion of the positive aspects along with the negative—even five times more positive than negative. (Chapter 3: Find the right crew.)

- Keep your eyes open through constant gathering of observations, inventories, and stories is called for. Gathering insights must welcome conversation and remember (even record) what has been observed. (Chapter 4: Gather insights through observation.)

- Reflecting on what has been seen must be recognized as a fundamental and real step in learning. Thinking time is essential for gaining the best insights. It demands more conversation and a willingness to allow for and even welcome conflicting perceptions. (Chapter 5: Equipping for the Dive.)

- It's scary to dive off the edge of the boat, yet there are gems to be found by exploring the water itself. This chapter helps you to see the potential of stepping out of your safe space and exploring beyond your normal boundaries, diving deep after new treasures. (Chapter 6, Learning the Lessons: Diving Deep.)

- Deciding about the next direction requires thinking about the lessons learned and what that means to your on-going plan for riding the current. When learning is tackled in this manner, a plan for assuring a safe and valuable journey almost defines itself. (Chapter 7, Taking Charge: Deciding what to do.)

- Lastly, learning opens up new worlds into which our curiosity draws us to continue our quest. (Chapter 8: Looking back and looking forward.)

Figure 1.1 places these 'voyage' concepts together to show what the learning process might look like. Each step is designed to create a good learning environment. As you go through the rest of this book, each of these steps will be expanded upon with more stories, specific exercises and actions that will prepare you for a great journey and successful quest.

Figure 1.1: The Voyage of the 'Knowledge Seeker' in Search of Fresh Knowledge

Be the Leader of Your Learning

You may or may not be a 'leader' in the formal sense. Your title may say nothing about taking initiative or leading others—but you are still the leader of your own learning. When I teach, I usually begin by saying to the participants that my job is to create a learning environment for them, where I will provide them with new information, knowledge and insights. It is up to them to decide what is relevant to them and what they will 'learn.' It's my way of saying that they are the leaders of their learning—even in a classroom.

Leading your own learning requires three essentials:
1. **Choose** to take some action.
2. Do some initial **assessment** of where you need or want to give attention.
3. Define the kind of **companions** you wish to bring to aid you in this work.

Let's look closer at each of these three essentials.

Choose Action – Lead Your Learning Quest

"Leadership is the ability to align strengths toward a goal or vision in such a way that weaknesses are irrelevant." Peter Drucker

Current knowledge enlivens everything it touches. Current knowledge keeps you interesting and more valuable to others—distinctive, able to move into new areas with greater ease, and able to contribute more effectively. Current knowledge also motivates you, the learner, to move to greater levels of attainment, in your specific work and in the world in general.

Making a choice takes energy, but it also provides energy. By choosing to take action—to be the leader of your learning quest

—you will find yourself energized for follow-through. (This energy is called *motivation* in management-speak.) You may be saying to yourself, "It's easy for you to talk about taking charge of my learning, but I live in a system that just won't change." Please continue reading. More is in your power to do than you may realize.

It doesn't matter what leads you to desire to improve your ability to keep your knowledge fresh—to **ride the current**. What does matter is that you decide to do so, setting out on a path that will lead to meaningful results. No matter what profession, craft or line of work you are in, knowledge is necessary, and **current** knowledge is essential.

Decide. Make it your choice. The resultant sense of empowerment leads to action, creating the changes needed to move toward accomplishment. When we invest our own energy in a decision, this energy grows with our commitment to the decision. Like a perpetual motion machine, choice energizes the actions needed to create the right environment for learning; the learning is likely to be successful, so the learner invests energy in learning more. It all begins with choice.

Assessment

We're each at a different place. Now that you have decided to ride the current, let's find the best place to launch your ship. Depending on where you are in your career or life, you will find different areas more or less important to you. Use this assessment instrument to discover which sections of this book have the most relevance for you in your current situation.Take the short self-assessment survey (Table 1.1) and 'launch' where it will be of most value to you.

Table 1.1 Assessment Instrument

Statement	Rate from 1 to 10	Areas where you might find help in this book	Potential Impact
I know the areas of knowledge where I wish to capitalize, keep current, or build.		Chapter 2 Selecting the Vessel	Keeps you interesting
I know the areas where my knowledge is strong. I know where I have made contributions to the knowledge of others.		Chapter 4 Stocking Supplies for the Journey	Keeps you valuable, distinctive
I have a strong support structure for my learning.		Chapter 3 Finding the Right Crew	Enlivens you
I have a colleague who regularly works with me to deepen my knowledge and understanding by helping me challenge my assumptions.		Chapter 4 Stocking Supplies for the	
I have someone who helps me see the bigger picture (of my industry, my workplace, the organization where I am employed) and how it relates to me and my areas of knowledge.		Journey Chapter 5 Equipping for the Dive	
I have regular opportunities for joining in conversations that help me enlarge my knowledge (virtual or face to face).			
I regularly seek out new areas to explore for new insights.		Chapter 6 Learning the Lessons: Diving Deep	Enlivens you, keeps you valuable

Statement	Rate from 1 to 10	Areas where you might find help in this book	Potential Impact
I regularly seek out new areas to explore for new insights.		Chapter 6 Learning the Lessons: Diving Deep	Able to move into new areas with greater ease.
I embrace ambiguity every chance I can get.		Chapter 6 Learning the Lessons: Diving Deep	Able to contribute more effectively to your life, your work, your world.
I can find most of the 'gems' I have found in the past and filed away.		Chapter 6 Learning the Lessons: Diving Deep	Able to move into new areas with greater ease.
I feel confident that I can capitalize on what I already know.		Chapter 6 Learning the Lessons: Diving Deep Chapter 7 Taking Charge: Deciding What to Do	Able to move into new areas with greater ease; able to contribute to the world in general.

Choice is Available

Pretend that you are walking in an unfamiliar city. You know roughly where you are, but not exactly, and you need to get to a meeting somewhere close by. You have a map in your briefcase; you have a cell phone with the number of the office where you are going to meet; and you see a friendly-looking stranger walking down the street toward you. Right now, make a decision. Decide if you will check the map, call the office, ask the stranger or continue trying by yourself to find the building where the meeting will be held. There is no right answer—it is just a matter of making a decision.

Just as you had choices in the imaginary scenario, at this moment, you do, too. You can continue to read this book hoping that it will help; you can stop reading this book and hope that it wouldn't have helped you anyway; or you can believe that this book will help you, and act on that belief to explore how to ride the current and then implement some or all of what you've learned.

Companions

Who would you like to join you as traveling companions on your voyage? In this book, several possibilities are offered. I will suggest you invite an *Accompanier*, described later in this chapter. This person goes with you, encourages you, supports you and offers information to which you may not have direct access. This could be a person who knows you well and encourages your growth. In an organizational setting, this Accompanier may be your boss. I will also suggest you invite a person you trust to help you think through what you are considering and learning. I call this person a *Practice Partner* and talk about what this partner does in Chapter 3. You are also welcome to assemble colleagues and friends who know you and can give you insights about your strengths. We'll talk more about how they help you develop your learning approach in Chapter 4.

The activities presented in this book can be done as a small group as well as individually. If you could entice a couple of friends to join you as fellow seekers after knowledge, the results will be enhanced through mutual support, not to mention expanded insights. Try to find one or two others who are willing to do the same exploration. Learning with others provides support and incentive to complete your individual part and gain the full benefits. Before you begin, are there others who might be willing to join you right now, set out on the same voyage, as you learn to ride the current?

How To 'Just Do It'

The upcoming chapters in this book offer the guidance you'll need for 'doing it'—learning to ride the current. You'll find a carefully chosen blend of theory and practical instructions. My approach is based on narrative practice, social constructionist concepts, Appreciative Inquiry, adult learning theory and the theories of group and thinking processes. It is solidly grounded in theory as well as years of experience and real-life examples of those who ride the current. The book will not spend a great deal of time on theory—only enough to provide a sufficient foundation for your thinking.

Each chapter will lead you through a series of explanations and examples conveying the actual experience and thinking of other people. Each will offer some preparatory exercises to set the stage and enhance your skills in what is about to come. Then each will present the actual steps you should take.

You may be tempted to just read the book. But if you are serious about learning to ride the current, taking on the quest, you will identify the sections that are of highest value to you and work through the exercises. It is through **experience** that the meaning becomes clearest for you. For example, when you are asked to interview others, don't shortchange yourself. Imagining what others will say is not the same as the exciting experience of actually hearing things you didn't expect—a key strategy of this approach. Do the work; conduct the interviews.

While I have chosen not to provide space for you to write your responses and notes in this book, I strongly recommend beginning this work with a tool to record what you are learning—a journal of some sort—perhaps as simple as a spiral-bound notebook or a steno pad. Just make sure that it is bound so that you can easily keep the notes together and in order. For some who are more attached to their computers, a computer program—as simple as Word or one more directed at content management such as Compendium—can be used. You might even decide to record your exercises and insights in a blog. The point is to be sure that you can organize the information from the start. The steps are presented in order and each has a given name. You might write the name of the step and the date at the top of the page where you are recording your thoughts and responses. In this way, you can always reconstruct your work.

Once you have decided to begin this work, take the Assessment (Table 1.1) and study the model (Figure 1.1) to decide where you will gain the highest return. However, unless you have answered the first question in the Assessment with a strong Yes, take the time to read and follow the exercises in Chapter 2: Designing the Vessel. Creating the framework (the boat of our metaphor) into which you will place your actions, decisions and lessons will keep you focused.

Early in your journey I suggest you give careful thought to your traveling companion which is discussed in Chapter 3: Finding the Right Crew. With the right vessel and crew, you can begin your voyage of discovery anywhere you wish, confident of finding treasure.

The Practice of 'Just Doing il'

"One can choose to go back toward safety or forward to growth. Growth must be chosen again and again; fear must be overcome again and again." Abraham Maslow

I remember the very first time I had to write a performance evaluation of one of my staff. That had to be one of the hardest things I ever did. I was asked to help an individual see where she needed to improve, along with telling her what she had done well. And in the end, I had to give her a score. I was incredibly uncomfortable. It felt so subjective. It felt so arbitrary. I didn't like the whole idea. In the end, I just did it.

Years later, after doing hundreds of performance evaluations, I have come to do them with ease. I still don't like the idea, but I have come to understand that my judgment is part of my job. Subjective as it may be, it comes with the territory of being a manager. The lesson had grown from doing the evaluation skillfully (the mental part), to becoming the coach who embodies the evaluation in a supportive manner (the emotional and physical part).

Dena Hawes tells a story of her decision to 'just do it.' "There was a huge learning curve that happened to me when I went to graduate school in Santa Barbara. I had waited eleven years before I went to graduate school. Up to then, I made jewelry. My identity was as a person who made things. I hardly opened a book. I read very little. I didn't see myself as a writer. I remember when I had to write my statement of interest in order to get into graduate school, I sat down, and I didn't know how to write."

"When I got [to graduate school], I…decided to become a good writer. I took a writing class and I really excelled in it. I even took a theory class. [Writing theory] is so complicated. I taped the lectures, I listened to them, I read over my notes. I was panicked. I thought I would fail the class. I did a lot of work—then suddenly it hit me."

"I wrote a review of an art exhibition, I sent it to the art critic at the newspaper, and I was hired by the paper. After that I just flourished. I loved to write."

Dena went on to say, "I made a real commitment to learn [how to write] because I made so many huge changes to go to graduate school… I felt I just can't fail." The decision to do it was the beginning of a great journey for Dena.

Even the hardest thing will become easier as you practice doing it. In the end, you learn more than you ever thought possible. Just decide to do it—and then follow through.

Deciding on Your Accompanier

As a curious person, I am always looking for new ideas and things to learn. If you saw my bookshelf, you would wonder why some of the topics have found their way there. You might be tempted to ask, "And why are you reading Dr. Seuss books?" But books are only a small part of where I seek learning.

I have a network of colleagues I go to because they have a known and different perspective from my own. I tend to call upon them during specific projects. I expect them to add to my reflections by showing an alternative point of view. I don't ask them to think with me, just offer their perspectives along the way. They join me on the journey at particular points, and I will be calling them in this book, my *Accompaniers*. I owe a lot to them. They play a major role in keeping my knowledge relevant. They are like travelers who have done a lot of traveling already and maybe to the same places I am headed.

While some people prefer to work alone, others, like me, really appreciate having another person to talk things over, ask advice, be encouraged and even challenged. Even if you like to work alone, you may want to find someone who will accompany you on this learning journey.

You should consider someone who knows you well and has encouraged you in the past. If you are working in an organization, you should consider asking the person you report to—your manager, boss, supervisor, team leader or whoever—to play this role. In either case, they can offer you the larger picture of the organization or field than you may be able to see from your perspective. And in this role, they will be asked to provide such information. Certainly your manager should have a greater perspective on how your work relates to the organization's goals. And this relationship is important to defend any request you may decide to make for time or resources.

If your search for knowledge finds you not part of an organization because you work independently or because you are in transition or you're a person just starting out, you will still find an accompanier valuable. What you will want in this person is someone who sees the larger picture of your life. For example, she may be an industry specialist in your field of interest. Perhaps he is a 'boomer' you feel knows you well and can help with your first steps as you start out.

Who you choose as your Accompanier is up to you. But note—if you work in an organization and you have a supervisor, there is a specific role for that person as well, independent of the Accompanier role – more about that later.
Each chapter will include instructions for the Accompanier including this one.

The Accompanier's Role:

Throughout the book, you'll find sections addressed to the Accompanier. No specific tasks are assigned to you at this time. However, if you enjoy the role of coach or mentor (neither are quite the same as an accompanier), you will find this new role fun and beneficial to yourself if you take time to study the role. If you have never played the role of coach or mentor, then you are in for a great experience as an accompanier.

If you are a supervisor, team member or a manager who is looking for a way to help those you work with, study of the Accompanier's role will benefit you, too. It will give you ideas on how to help those who have chosen to purposefully search for current knowledge themselves. It will also give you ideas on how you might work with your entire team to develop and freshen their knowledge together.

If you are concerned that this role will interfere with your supervisory role, be at ease. Just think of all the things you do in a day that are not directly related to your role as supervisor to your staff. You are already playing the role of accompanier when you attend meetings where a staff member does the presentation, or you introduce staff to key players in their work whom they should meet. In both of these situations, you are playing the role of Accompanier. As an Accompanier, you will do those tasks that only you can do and leave the rest to others.

That said, there are several levels at which you may find yourself involved—not at all, to a minimal degree, somewhat or fully as an Accompanier. Let's look at what each of these means.

Not at All: I probably don't have to explain this one. If the individual is doing the work of this book totally for his own personal or professional goals, then he may not find it useful for you to be a part of it. However, the exercises include interviewing someone who evaluates the work of the learner. So, at some point, you may be involved. At that point, your responsibility is to be honest in the interview and to encourage the individual's desire to enhance his professional life.

To a Minimal Degree: The individual may want you to be aware of what she is doing so you will understand some of the activities she will be doing. This is practically the same as 'Not at All' but with the refinement that the individual actually wants you to know what she is doing.

Somewhat: The individual learning to ride the current may prefer to seek some help from you, even if she is quite capable of proceeding. For example, she may ask for recommendations on those to interview. If she is early in her career, this is a reasonable strategy but not essential.

Fully: This is the situation where the individual asks you to be his or her Accompanier. The role is not demanding, but it does ask that you be available at times. If you are asked, check the sections addressed to the Accompanier so that you can anticipate your role and responsibilities.

These sections are plainly marked: Accompaniers. They are placed on the second page of each chapter and are presented in this type of box. These sections will guide you on how to support your staff. You should be a welcome guest to the conversation when everyone knows your role as well as their own.

If You Are a Boss and Decide This Approach is Something You Wish for Your Staff

As supervisor or manager, you might decide to request that staff use the approach of this book to develop their own plans for remaining current as part of a larger strategy for the unit, a career development strategy, or perhaps just a general improvement of the team. If this is the case, read the entire book with emphasis on the sections addressed to the Accompaniers. Then be sure that you and the staff member(s) or the team come to an agreement about how much involvement they desire and need, and what evidence will be necessary to demonstrate completion of their work on their plans. This is an important step! Once you have agreed on what completion will look like, stand ready to be available to do your role.

In all cases, keep your eye on the sections for the Accompaniers. They are placed on the second page of each chapter and are presented in this type of box. These sections will guide you on how to support your staff. You should be a welcome guest to the conversation when everyone knows your role as well as their own.

Using This Book, Doing This Work

We work best when we can see clearly what we need to do. For that reason, I end each chapter with specific sections designed to make next steps (and the reason to do them) clear.

In most chapters, you will find a section that explains how Accompaniers might fulfill their role. These sections are headed 'For the Accompanier.'

Near the end of each chapter is a section labeled 'Expected results/outcomes' that gives the rationale for each recommended action, tying the practical steps to the underlying foundation of my approach.

At the conclusion of each chapter you'll find sections headed 'Record and reflect', 'Possible Options' and 'Lessons Learned'. When you reach these sections—before you go further—record your possible options for action and your lessons learned. Take a moment to focus what you've just taken in, relating new learning to your previous understanding of how you keep your knowledge fresh and alive.

I encourage you to state your plans in positive phrases, using active verbs. I will prompt you to write one to six action steps. I'll remind you to pick one to incorporate into your work starting the next day.

Have you made the choice to begin learning to ride the current? Have you completed the assessment in Table 1.1, to determine which chapters of the book are of most value to you? Then it's time for you to begin.

Record and Reflect

Whether you've chosen to use a spiral bound journal, a notebook, a computer program, a blog or some other tool, start at the beginning and state your decision to do this. Write it out clearly in the form of a complete sentence, and include the date. Put this book down. Start writing down your thoughts and actions now.

Figure 1.2: Excerpts from Madelyn's Journal

Lessons: The idea of doing something active about keeping myself current is most appealing. My clients have always valued my contributions when I can bring them information and ideas that are up to date, clear, and relevant to them. But they particularly value the up to date. It gives them a sense of being more up to date themselves. Thus, pursuing this project of creating my own plan for riding the current feels both useful for me and valuable to my client work. I'm going to do it.

Action: I've decided to record my findings, lessons, and actions in an electronic file. I'll ...

Possible Options

At this point, with this chapter fresh in your mind, it's time to capture your ideas about actions you might take. Get them down in writing now.

Is every action you write down a commitment to follow through? No! That would be overwhelming, and not truly productive. A better idea is to consider these *possible options*. At the point you feel complete with your work of learning to ride the current, you will be ready to choose from these possible options the actions that are right for you—and in what sequence. Start writing down possible options for action now.

To get you started, let me ask—Have you invited anyone to be your Accompanier? If not, what's stopping you? Exploring that will be a very important action for you.

 ## Lessons Learned

This chapter has focused on helping you make the decision to begin learning to ride the current. What fresh knowledge is yours, now that you've read the chapter and completed the self-assessment tool? What have you learned about learning? Write down your observations now.

Riding The Current

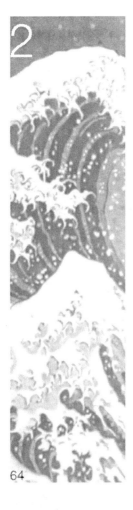

Simple, clear purpose and principles give rise to complex and intelligent behavior. Complex rules and regulations give rise to simple and stupid behavior.
~ Dee Hock

Selecting the Vessel

"We can't start without constraints, because that's chaos. We need to find out what are the minimum specs, the fundamental rules that we will share so that we can both support the key needs of the organization and at the same time make it easy for surprises to happen, for the unknown to emerge creatively. That's a liberating structure!"~Lisa Kimball, one of the founders of the concept and creation of virtual communities.

Graduating lawyers struggle to pass the Bar exam. Many times I have heard one say to me that he had to take it more than once before he could pass even though he had studied and studied. In addition to years in law school, there are special classes for preparing lawyers for this test, but they don't guarantee a passing grade. There is something more to passing the Bar exam.

Then I met Kathy Clark, a California lawyer who works in collaborative law around the country. She went to law school at age 39 and took the Bar in 1988. She says that she wasn't a good

The Accompanier's Role: Provide Information

Setting boundaries will be hard for most people, but it is the essential first step toward developing and implementing a personal knowledge approach. It is essential to do this step thoughtfully and from a well-informed position. As the Accompanier, you can perform three roles:

1. Provide information the person cannot get for himself,
2. Support the individual's decision-making process (without taking charge of it) and
3. Encourage the individual with nonjudgmental enthusiasm.

Your role as an Accompanier reflects your relationship to the individual you are accompanying. Is this someone who is redefining their life's goals? Is this someone who is starting out his career and not yet working? Is this someone who is seeking to enhance his avocation or enjoyment of life? You can help by sharing stories with the learner of your relevant experiences. You can help by matching the learner's goals to those of the field, the industry, or society.

Is this someone you supervise? If so, you can help her understand the link between her service in her work unit and the organization's objectives. Do you share a role as team members with this person? You can help her see the needs of the team from your perspective. Are you a colleague, doing similar work at a similar level, in the same organization or elsewhere? You can help the person you are accompanying see the larger picture. It's always hard to see the forest when you are among the trees. The Accompanier has the perspective to step out of the trees to get a better look.

For this step, Accompanier, your task is to provide the information your learner needs—always in full recognition that the choice of container is her decision. For the learner, a hard part of this step is likely to be linking what she wants to do with the bigger trends or the business goals and objectives. Your help in interpreting the impact of this choice is likely to be valuable if the individual doesn't have the maturity or scope to see the larger picture. Your role will be to help this person assess her ability to understand this and to fill in the gaps.

If you have helped the individual decide to develop her own plan for keeping knowledge fresh, then you have a responsibility to provide necessary information and links. This is not a blame game where you can say, "But I provided you with all the tools. Why come to me for anything?" It's time to support her process. Don't scrimp on the information you give.

It is essential that the individual make her own decisions at this stage. This is part of the organic nature of the work. Your job is to support this process, not do it **for** the individual. Offer information and support while respecting the decisions made by the person. To do this well, ask questions. When you have a point to make, turn it into a question so that the learner can discover it for herself.

Making the choice of container is challenging; it can't be done half-heartedly. Please be an encourager, not a provider of the decision. Making decisions is inherently energizing. The individual you accompany will need that energy as fuel for the journey ahead.

General objectives for the Accompanier:
- Assure that the individual understands what the larger goals mean in relation to her current position, station in life, place (she needs to begin with the right linkage here).
- Offer to review the individual's final list of topics and explore why she has selected them. (Make no

judgment of the topics selected. Merely help her explore
her rationale for choosing each. That is part of learning—
yours, too.)
- Offer encouragement to pursue the development and
  implementation of her plan.
- Ask questions that will help her examine why she is
  doing this.

Specific help the Accompanier provides:
- If the seeker's plan is career-related, provide relevant
  business goals and objectives at the industry,
  organization, unit and individual level.
- If her plan is not career-related, provide relevant trends
  as you see them.
- Ask which of the exercises presented in this chapter the
  individual has decided to do. (Your interest and
  encouragement indicate the importance of the
  exercises.)
- Offer to discuss the lessons the individual has learned
  from the exercises. (This is strictly optional, but useful if
  you have the time).

student in college, but decided to become a lawyer because of her
vision of doing some public service work. How she was going to
do this came from reading the book *Transforming Practices* by
Steve Keeva. In his book, Keeva says that lawyers were originally
healers. They were educated people in the community who could
bring healing by sitting down and mediating between two people.
Reading the book, she realized that "lawyers are healers" and there
is a world of people who are doing this kind of law. "As lawyers,
we walk out almost with a suit of armor. After reading his book, I
saw there are a lot of people going in a new direction."

Today, she does contract work for a firm in San Francisco
that allows her to serve the public practicing collaborative law,

which begins with the idea that a legal conflict can become a
healing moment when all the parties are in the room to just talk.

But Kathy's story is most relevant to us because of how she
was able to become a practicing lawyer. Kathy Clark passed the
Bar exam on the first try. Here's her story about how she studied
for it and how this 'habit' has been integrated into her approach
toward her lifelong pursuit of knowledge.

She explained, "When I studied for the Bar, I went to the
classes to help you prepare for them. The classes are four hours
each, four times a week, for eight weeks. I never took a note.
Everyone around me was saying, 'You're not taking any notes!' I
thought I would be less anxious and able to learn more if I just sat
and listened. It wasn't that I didn't have notes to study from the
rest of the time, but sitting in the class it felt very freeing to me to
just listen. I heard a lot more than I would have if I had done what
is standard in my life—take a lot of notes. All that did was sort of
jumble up things in my head. I don't know why I decided to try it.
I'm usually very distractible and not focused, but when I studied
for the Bar exam, I was incredibly focused. For eight weeks, I did
nothing but think about it, sit in class, and go through the whole
thing in my mind with various scenarios. When I went into the
exam, I knew I had done everything I could do. I went feeling like
a whole person. I came to it very calm. I had the wherewithal to
figure this all out and it worked. It really worked for me!"

Today, when Kathy attends conferences, she continues this
habit of being free of note taking. She sits with no pens or paper
around her and just listens.

Kathy had a clear goal in mind—pass the Bar. But she also
had the framework in mind that permitted her to let the lessons she
was hearing fit in automatically, relating new information to what
she already knew. This freed her to think, to integrate the
lessons, to relate the lessons to situations rather than the

details. The specific goal and the existing framework gave her clarity, and clarity focuses the mind. In this case, the framework and the goal were mutually supporting. They formed a container in which Kathy could learn with great ease. The container in which we operate truly makes a difference.

The First Steps

Kathy had a single, clear goal — pass the Bar. You will need to answer the question: what is my goal for keeping my knowledge fresh? For some of you, answering this question is simple and easy. You have thought about this before and know exactly why you are pursuing a life of ongoing learning. For others, knowing exactly where to go is uncertain. Perhaps you are young in your life and would like to wait for more exposure before making up your mind. Or perhaps you have a mind that so thoroughly enjoys exploring all kinds of topics that making a decision about which ones doesn't feel right for you. In these cases, your challenge will be more difficult — and maybe more interesting.

I suggest that at the least, you state a goal to yourself that you want to remain open to possibilities. Obviously, you'll need a vessel that can change itself the moment you find a target of interest. If this sounds impossible, you will learn later that your vessel can have adjustable and even permeable sides. In fact, in later chapters, you will meet those who go beyond adjusting their vessel and jump ship altogether. But for now, the key is to be clear to yourself about your immediate desire so that you can begin this journey.

Once you know where you want to go, the second question is, What knowledge is the most important to me? What existing framework of knowledge do you already possess that you plan to use for sifting and sorting? You will only be able to store and use the new information you gain when you can relate the new to what you already know. Just as Kathy used her existing knowledge of the law for her framework, what will be yours? The framework you choose should reflect the knowledge that is important to you along with the experiences you have had in life.

Together, your existing framework of important knowledge and the goal(s) you set yourself for keeping your knowledge current will make up the container (the vessel) of this journey.

It turns out that the view of what is important, what the ultimate goal should be, depends on whether you must respond to demands that push you or challenges that pull you toward them. The first is the push of normal, everyday demands of life, the job, your field, the business. Are you concerned about paying the mortgage, keeping up your license, remaining competitive? In these cases the container is likely to be some aspect(s) of your field that has highest relevance to the goal of maintaining your life, your job, your business.

The second is the pull that feels almost like a calling. The call may be coming from systemic aspects of your field, the interaction of your field with another, that naturally draw you beyond the edges of your field into other fields. For example, in the field of management, there is a natural interaction between management theory and organizational psychology. In botany, there is a natural link to genetics. The pull is to reach beyond your field into a 'neighboring' field. Alternatively, the pull of a challenge may be from the depths of your field, challenging you to reach even deeper. You may become so passionate about your area that nothing will satisfy you but to dive deeper and deeper into its unknown. In responding to a challenge by stepping beyond or deeply into the field, there must always be a lifeline—a large, solid foundation of knowledge already obtained from which you can reach out and relate new knowledge that is being discovered and drawn in.

The container or vessel built in response to these

calls may be quite different from the container built in response to the push of demands. Whether your calling is drawing you toward breadth, exploration of what lies beyond the horizon, or depth, exploration of what lies deep beneath the surface, that calling must be reflected in the vessel you choose to carry you as you go. Moreover, those venturing into neighboring areas or diving deep will require permeable and even adjustable sides (boundaries). But even for those who are responding to the demands of life, there are likely to be changes in their containers over time. This journey is anything but a straight line.

Examples From Those Who've Felt the Push and Pull

I'd like you to hear what a few of my interview subjects had to say when asked about the pushes and pulls that affect their choice of vessel as they seek to keep their knowledge fresh.

Some described dealing with demands that push. Marsha Scorza, a licensed professional elementary school counselor, says, "I must keep my license up to date. This drives my selections." The owner of a manufacturing plant, Rodger Whipple, uses a different measure, saying that he focuses on those topics that "keep costs down and make my company more competitive." "It's the mortgage that keeps me focused, but I'd love the additional luxury to pick a new or related field of study and go back for another advanced degree," says a career civil servant, Fred Dogget. "There are areas I want to concentrate on, and then there's the idea of being employed," says Cait Cusack, a medical doctor working in research.

Others among my interviewees described the pull of challenges that draw them toward other fields. For some, their work or their vision of their work is very broad. Playwright and director Christopher Heimann has to work constantly between radically different arenas. He says this involves "keeping current in the field of science—knowing how the mind works—and a mixture of the ancient stuff—human behaviors of actors." Rick Weldon, Maryland State Representative, says, "I am driven by my interests that are also of interest to my constituencies." These individuals seem to be on a bridge that stretches between two places—the wide demands of their work and the deep demands of their interests.

Sometimes the stretch is done with ease. "I find the open-endedness around conflict resolution to be the same as that around performance art, which are two fields I brought together. Performance art is literally undefinable. It defies definition, because you can't pin it down. It's that kind of art that is blurring art and life. It permeates into all different disciplines and areas of study and parts of life. The two areas, conflict resolution and performance art, are my two areas where I want to remain 'with it,'" says Dena Hawes, a mid-career professional artist and recent PhD graduate in conflict resolution.

"I'm not sure I can ever zero in. I have a rather wide filter. I need to look at the periphery and the unknowns that would be missed if I zeroed in," says learning coach and technologist, Claudia L'Amoreaux.

Among the people I interviewed who feel pulled by challenges, some are drawn toward going deeply into their chosen passion, rather than exploring the space between fields. For these people, the decisions around where to keep one's knowledge fresh and alive take on new dimensions. For the renowned voice coach, Howard Milner, the choice is depth. He says, "The principles [in music] become simpler, but the understanding of what the words mean deepens. So the story remains the same but what it means, changes. It's the same ingredients, but it becomes a different dish."

Listen to how Laura Woods-Nokes, a recent A Level graduate in England, (which relates roughly and not

perfectly to a high school graduate of the U.S.) describes how she selects her studies. "I chose a subject that I found hard to do. Therefore, I would find it most rewarding because I would struggle with it, and it would mean something more to me."
These examples show that creating a container for knowledge-seeking is a constant matter of close observation of the chosen field, by scanning the horizon, plumbing the depths, or both.

These people function on the edges of their field and sometimes over the edge, yet they feel no hesitancy to be there. There is no reluctance in making this choice, even when it is hard to do.

Regardless of where you find yourself—pushed by demands or pulled by challenges, exploring the bridge between disciplines or the diving into the depths within one specialty—you have choices. You set your own goals (where you wish to seek the treasure) and design the appropriate vessel (fitted to the needs of the journey) for pursuing the treasure of current knowledge. Without a good vessel, you risk achieving nothing.

Why a Vessel? The Benefits of Constraints

A paradox is fundamental to holistic thinking: you can't have freedom without some constraint, they are two parts of the same whole." ~ Glory Ressler, award-winning consultant from Canada.

The key is narrowing. I use my interests and what's exciting. The hardest thing is to decide what you won't do." ~ *Ralph Scorza, scientist*

Why spend time talking about the vessel—the container that holds your search within chosen boundaries?

The scope of all things known is enormous. Just to comprehend its vastness is difficult if not impossible. Yet this is the universe in which we must make our decisions about remaining current. We've seen that setting goals directs our thinking. Thinking about and making choices about the knowledge we feel is most important to our goals creates a container or vessel for pursuing our goals. And while the container may have adjustable sides, the sides are boundaries that define a space in which we can operate. The definition of the space facilitates focus and enhances efficiency. With a defined area in which to work, you don't have to expend energy again and again in answering the question, Where is the limit?

I coach people who are world-renowned in particular subject areas. My coaching is about helping them convey their knowledge to an audience less expert in the field. I always begin my coaching session by asking my clients, "What do you want to accomplish?" I have to ask this question three times before they get the message that I am not talking about the substance of their talk, but rather about their intentions for the session. At this point, I have been told things like, "I want them to use this model in their projects." Or, more simply, "I don't want anyone to leave during my talk." Whatever it is, this becomes the focus and container for the rest of our conversation. With clear focus, we get to work on creating the right learning environment for their listeners to achieve the speaker's intentions. I could coach them on many things, but by creating a container for our work together, we both achieve success.

In one case, the individual felt that there was nothing I could add to his presentation because I did not know his subject. Once we identified his real intentions for the session, I set those intentions as the container for my work with him. All my comments were directed at helping him achieve his intentions, rather than helping him with the content of his presentation. He quickly saw that here, he could learn. He allowed himself to listen with an open mind to the techniques I introduced for achieving his intentions. Focusing only on this aspect (intentions) allowed me to go into depth. He was able within a short time to grasp the concepts and techniques I was offering and achieve exactly what he wanted in his presentation.

Why the Container Matters

You may be feeling still that a container represents unacceptable limits. I contend the boundaries of your container offer freedom. Let me explain.

There are people who avoid setting boundaries because they feel their freedom will be taken away from them if they set them. Then there are people who feel they are so bright, they do not need boundaries. Of course, there are people who simply don't want to make the effort to define the container. Alternatively, there are some who are still searching for their own identity as they are very young, early in their career, or simply just that kind of person. They feel drawn to whatever is around them instead of being able to make the decision for themselves. For them, this ability to choose what knowledge is most important (or even to set their own goals) may be a particular challenge. My advice is to make a temporary choice, recognizing that it will change over time. This may be seen as a weakness by some, but in fact, it gives you a certain strength in being open and malleable. These are prime characteristics of the mind in learning mode.

Regardless of which of these types you identify with, you should appreciate the actual effects of having no container—the loss of focus, lack of depth, inefficiency, and even the loss of freedom to perform well.

Some people embrace containers because they see that the container is linked to efficiency in learning. The boundaries of the container focus the learner so he knows when he is making progress and when he has reached goals—both important to being efficient.

Then there are those who see the careful selection of containers as a way to assure their learning will be more effective. Accepting boundaries allows learners to feel a real sense of freedom to pursue and explore, knowing the limitations reflect personal desires serving professional and life goals. These learners experience a sense of playfulness even as they pursue their goals. They are experiencing freedom as an effect of their container.

A container is not a prison—it's a vessel designed to help you travel efficiently and effectively.

The Vice President and the Fence

Containers can be **efficient**. A corporate vice president bemoaned that he could never give a task force freedom to define the solution to a problem because it would recommend something that simply would not work. When asked why, he claimed they didn't have the broader understanding, the wider view. I suggested that he define the task with a set of objectives designed to take into account existing constraints that would focus the efforts of the task force, and thus allow them to come up with a solution that was acceptable. (I likened this to a fenced in back yard that allowed children to play safely within it.) He got the point. The job of laying out the container along with the goal was his to do. The task force was then free to discover a solution that met the container requirements (which he had set) and use their creative talents to the full to achieve the goal. He realized this was the approach he needed to take and did so to his complete satisfaction. This does not mean that it was easy for him to define the container. It meant that he recognized his own responsibility while offering a real opportunity for his staff to 'play' and create something really great and new.

If you are still thinking of boundaries as too limiting, consider the example of a PhD candidate who is trying to write a dissertation. Her mind moves out and out, and the dissertation gets bigger and bigger. Suddenly the candidate, in an attempt to cover an impressive amount of territory, is overwhelmed with the breadth of the topic. Lacking the experience or training to create her own limits, she needs her advisor to impose discipline and focus the topic to a targeted goal. With that help, not only is her dissertation more likely to be successful, depth within the topic becomes possible. She has moved from feeling imprisoned by her boundless surroundings to feeling free to begin an efficient and effective writing process, working within a well-chosen container.

No one I know argues against setting goals, but many clamor when I suggest that with goals come limits. They get over it when I explain that limits change; they grow or shrink, are permeable, and disappear when the goal is achieved. Limits are meant to serve goals, not frustrate achievement. Limits are the container. Setting goals and boundaries—and accepting the limits that come with them—are a necessary part of your approach to keeping your knowledge fresh.

If you were going to collect water, you would certainly want a container—big enough to carry a sufficient supply, but not so big that you can't lift it full. If you were setting out on a voyage, you would appreciate the vessel that keeps you contained and dry, steering toward your chosen compass point. If you are building an approach for keeping your knowledge fresh, it will need some focus and direction. This is how you avoid becoming overwhelmed, unable to make decisions, or confused. And if decisions and confusion are not the issue for you, consider the possibility that your learning may become too diffused—unrelated to your base of knowledge. Diffused learning may prevent you from recognizing lessons or relating them to what you know. So, pick a container that is big enough to hold your dreams and goals, but not so big you can't carry it.

Designing Your Vessel: Preparatory Exercises

The following exercises will help you firmly establish in your mind what a container is, before you begin to design one for yourself.

The first exercise is required, followed by nine more optional exercises. Read through the optional ones and decide which relate best to you. Choose at least **two or three** from exercises 2 through 10 to complete.

Required:

1. Take a moment now and think about where you are in the story in your life. What has brought you to this point, where you are asking yourself to consider better management of your own knowledge? Are you in the early stages of your career and need to focus directly on the demands of the work at hand, or are you feeling drawn to the edge by the challenges there? Who formed your ideas about what and how to study? Do you still hear their voices in the back of your mind? Are these ideas still working for you? Take a moment now and write your story down. Don't worry if it doesn't look like a story. Just take the time to think about the questions I've posed, and your thoughts about them.

Optional:

2. Think of a time when you hit something totally new

and unexpected—a time when your immediate response was to reject the premise. Stop: what assumptions were you making about that thing that triggered your rejection?

3. Consider a time when you thought of a new way to do something but found that you could not act on it. Stop: What was holding you back? Try to define it.

4. Think of a time when you were working in a team with a vague goal. Stop: What would have made the goal clearer to you?

5. Consider a time when you were giving an assignment to someone else. Now, write up the assignment so well that the person can do the job with nothing more than the written description. Stop: (1) Have you defined the goal of what needs to be done or have you defined how to achieve it? (2) Could the person create her own plan with creativity or will she be required to follow the steps you have laid out in order to achieve the goal?

6. Boundaries sometimes are best understood when we suspend them. Imagine a world where there is no friction. Take some time to describe how it would look and what would be different in that world.

7. Think of your work and the mandate or mission statement of your organization. How do you use this mandate or mission to decide whether you will take on a task? Imagine how you might change the mission statement to offer you greater freedom of action. Imagine how you might change the mission statement to restrict actions.

8. What laws facilitate you doing your business? Consider laws of society and those of nature. Pay particular attention to those that constrain your actions or define boundaries.

9. What rules in your organization unnecessarily restrict how people act? How would you change them to allow more freedom of action but still meet the mission and spirit of the rule?

10. If you are in a team, how has the team defined its working relationships? Are the ground rules around working relationships working? Why? What encourages members to follow the ground rules? What about them restricts action (good or bad)?

Remember, your task is to complete the first exercise, then choose and complete the two or three optional exercises that relate best to your current situation.

In the early nineteenth century, scientists believed that electricity flowed through a wire as water through a pipe. Michael Faraday thought that he "saw" a flow **around** a wire that was conducting electricity. (A wire conducting electricity induces a magnetic field around the wire.) The idea of electricity having any influence or form outside the wire was inconceivable at the time. The assumption that electricity was inside the wire flowing like water was so strong that it took many years and much evidence to prove their assumptions (their boundaries) were wrong. In 1831 Faraday demonstrated the principle of induction—electricity not only influences space outside the wire, electricity is created by moving wires through lines of magnetic force. Today's generators and electric motors are based on this.

 ## Designing Your Vessel: Action Exercises

Like the treasure hunter, you need to begin with the reason for seeking treasure. In other words, you need to keep the end result in mind. You need to define your longer-term goals. Think about why a treasure hunt is important at all.

This book is not about defining your life goals or mission — the longer-term goals mentioned above. Life goals are presented well and with many exercises in other books. For example, *The Seven Habits of Highly Effective People* by Steven Covey contains wonderful exercises for this exploration. For those who are not attracted to 'highly effective,' there is *How to Discover Your Personal Mission* by John Monbourquette, a book that walks the reader through an entire process with gentleness and great examples.

That said, you are now commencing a step that follows setting life goals. Having mapped out what you want to accomplish in the long run, you need to determine what you want to accomplish in the short run of the work you are doing with this book. This short-term goal-setting is about establishing the range of topics that you feel are important to serve your life goals or mission. It's easy to see how choosing topics applies to creating your container.

But where to begin? First, decide if serving business needs is to be a part of this. I suspect it will be in many cases. (By the way, I don't distinguish between profit, nonprofit, family or government when I use the word *business*.) This is about succeeding in your business setting. You are preparing yourself to succeed at work through an improved learning approach that serves the needs of the business.

Many of you will be more interested in the pursuit of fresh knowledge that serves your personal goals. Some of you will incorporate both aspects — business and personal — at this point. The good news is that topics that are of interest to you personally will serve to bring perspective to your thinking in the areas of business. (I'll return to this topic in later chapters.) So in any case, feel free to list personal as well as professional (work-related) topics.

Your actions, then, will be to:

- Find a methodology for setting your personal goals or mission if that is important to you at this time.
- Talk to your supervisor, manager or key client to see if you truly understand the business needs to which you contribute. This will be a great way to prepare him or her for your later request for an interview. (For those of you who work for yourselves, this is a great opportunity to talk to your clients.)
- Explore the trends in your profession, field, and/or industry.
- List your hobbies and interests and indicate the ones that you actually spend time doing.
- Establish an initial set of boundaries for yourself and this work of creating your personal knowledge plan.
- Review the thoughts and stories you read at the opening of this chapter. Think about the impact of those on your boundaries. Are you now more aware of your assumptions?

Write down your impressions after completing each of the above actions. Review your notes, then indicate which of the points seem to offer the best boundaries for your work of knowledge-seeking. Write down your short-term goals for the activity of keeping your knowledge fresh, and the topics/areas you will include.

By completing these actions, you define your goal and initial set of boundaries—the destination and design for your vessel. You will find yourself revisiting this list as you continue your exploration, customizing your learning approach, through other chapters of this book.

You will be learning a lot just in pursuing this process. As you learn, you will push at the boundaries or, perhaps, withdraw from one of them. Don't be alarmed by this. Organic processes (which we talked about in Chapter 1) often loop back on themselves. They remain flexible and produce new insights, even when revisiting old terrain.

An occasional review will happen naturally, is supposed to happen, and is valuable. The recursive nature is built into this process, and you will want to allow yourself the freedom to learn about learning as you learn about other things. A question asked a second time always gives you more.

Setting wide boundaries can bring clarity. Years ago I participated in a personal development program and learned that my goal in life was to help people grow—easy to say, hard to do. This happened about the time I began my consulting practice. Figure 2.2 depicts selections from my journal pages as I worked the exercises in this chapter.

 Expected Results/Outcomes

From this step, you should have an initial list of boundary statements:
- Personal goals
- Business needs to which you contribute and are likely to serve to build your career
- Professional goals for yourself
- Trends that influence your work
- Areas of strong personal interest that appear to refresh you

Together these form the design of the vessel we've been talking about. You now have a "blueprint" to constrain your knowledge seeking, so that it is as efficient, useful, profound, and liberating as you want it to be. Don't revisit your vessel's design over and over again, but do expect this design phase to reoccur, when the need to do so appears organically.

In Chapter 1, I introduced the concept of the Accompanier —a person you invite along on your voyage, who encourages you, supports you and offers information. In Chapter 3, I have more to say on choosing the Accompanier, as part of finding the right crew for the trip. As the knowledge-seeker addresses designing the vessel, the Accompanier can be of great help. If you have selected an Accompanier, invite him or her to read the sidebar on the Accompanier's role. Each subsequent chapter includes similar sidebars for Accompaniers to read.

Record and Reflect

Review what you have written as you completed the Preparatory Exercises and Action Exercises. Record in your journal the list of the points that seem the best container for your plan. Remember, it doesn't matter if you've chosen to use a journal, notebook, computer program, blog or some other tool. Just pick what works for you and do it. Start writing down your thoughts and actions now.

Figure 2.2: Excerpts From Madelyn's Journal

understood more about organizations as human systems. All the time I was a division chief at the World Bank, I never felt I had the time to read or go to classes or workshops or conferences.

day management. I found myself designing complex research projects that led to clear results, defendable conclusions and natural actions. At last, I found that learning in classes is only the start.

Learning about the theoretical background behind what I had learned through my own....

I find that I am able to draw from this reservoir of knowledge and experience at a moment's notice so long as I keep my eyes open to what is happening around me and keep the confidence in my own knowledge high....

Trends I see that are important to me are:
- Growing need to be both efficient and effective in a global economy...

Professional: to remain current in the fields that support the services I offer to my clients.
- Management theory
- Current Events especially international...

practice rather than study it. Painting, an old love, had to go, too. It lurks in the corners of my mind, however.

Possible Options

After you've reviewed your work from this chapter, brainstorm a list of actions you might take to define your goals and design your vessel. You may choose to do all the preparatory and action exercises now, or decide to keep reading, holding those as future options for action.

Remember, you're not committing to undertake **now** each action you write down—you're creating a list of possible options. As you move forward, customizing your own approach to riding the current, you will revisit the list at the end of each chapter and create your action plan.

Lessons Learned

In this chapter I've focused on helping you answer the question, What knowledge is the most important to you? I've given you exercises designed to help you establish boundaries that keep you learning efficiently and effectively, focused on a field of inquiry, able to determine which treasures to keep and where to put them in relation to what you already know.

This is a good time to review your notes on this chapter, and also to review the self-assessment tool presented in Chapter 1. Will you be moving from this chapter to Chapter 3, Finding the Right Crew? If you are not working through the book sequentially, what chapter is right for you to move to next? What have you learned that you would like to record for use in that next step? Write down your observations now.

Riding The Current

3

Finding the Right Crew

Bob Sadler has a great story about how he engages colleagues in his crew as he rides the current. Today Bob works with high-tech clients in Silicon Valley. He started his career teaching English.

"I loved teaching and did some organizing in low income neighborhoods." His students lived in a tough neighborhood, and Bob spent 10 years helping the neighborhood build itself up. He developed a consensus of vision among community leaders, bankers and others, and then mobilized people to achieve the vision. "As I got better and better at this, the businesses in the neighborhood asked if I would deploy in their companies. There are ghettos in companies where the need is to bring people and work groups together. It was foreign to me, but it worked. Eventually, I morphed into a business consultant working with Change Management, and I have done this ever since."

The Accompanier's Role: Demonstrate Support

As an Accompanier, your job is to help the learner feel comfortable talking with you even to the point of being willing to 'stick her neck out.' Your job is to keep your mind open and curious as a model for the learner, and so support her through example. Your job is to keep your eye on both the gain the person will achieve in working this approach, and your own gain in being a part of this work. It should not feel like a burden to you. If it does, ask to be relieved!

If you are a manager or supervisor and have assigned this book and its approach to your team, the team should discuss this step and decide as a team if they will serve as each other's Practice Partners. The activities you do at this stage with the team are the same as for an individual. Pose the questions to the team and ask each to respond.

This chapter has talked about the value of an appreciative approach to the activities. Be sure that you understand what this means and that you are able to be appreciative to the seeker.

Today, Bob spends his time on large-scale collaborative events such as one- to four-day workshops with upwards of one hundred people trying to create a new future. He says, "I focus on how to design agendas that are fresh, fast, thorough, robust—so that time spent is well spent." The other part of Bob's work is executive coaching, where he is constantly looking for psychological and social systems to gather data on people and teams of people. The focus is on finding where their strengths are and making them more effective. "I'm always trying new instruments, testing new approaches that show promise."

Bob's story becomes still more intriguing when he talks about how he stays current. "I don't learn through study," he says. "I have an enormous network of friends and colleagues which I have had for long years! I talk constantly. And all of these people are active in the same fields, know things I haven't heard of. They are quick to share and pick up ideas. I do go to week-long immersion workshops and work to meet all the participants. I don't take notes or read, but I get what I learn from people. I don't read business books, ever. I read really good fiction only. Good fiction gives insights into human interactions."

When Bob went on his own as a consultant, he invited friends to a hotel, and they each took turns talking about what they were doing and what was working. This led to three more meetings and the group grew to twenty people. Today, most of the networking time is on a phone call or over coffee or dinner. Bob says he learns more from colleagues than clients. "Most clients are stuck five to twenty years behind the curve. I get paid for bringing the world to them. I learn four or five times more from colleagues who are cross-pollinating and improving what they are doing. Moreover, my social networks offer me love and affection, which provides the underpinnings of confidence. Knowledge alone won't do this."

Bob discovered a strategy for engaging the right crew to help him ride the current. When you have finished the work of this chapter, you will have your strategy. You'll be ready to invite on your journey the right crew to create and support a comfortable learning climate for you.

Why a Seeker Needs Partners

"It's very easy to burrow in and do my work. I have to force myself to contact my friends. It quadruples my knowledge when I listen, and I have plenty of friends for that."-Larry Prusak

In Chapter 1, I somewhat facetiously referred to you as the 'Captain of the Knowledge Seeker.' I drew the connection between the right ship and the right crew (among other assets) in seeking treasure, be it sunken gold or fresh knowledge. Who you surround yourself with on this journey has much to do with the success of your voyage.

Bob's story says a lot about how powerful competent colleagues can be in riding the current. Moreover, the colleagues have clearly become friends as well. They make themselves available to him and give emotional support—essential characteristics of this fellowship. Notice how these characteristics come as a package.

Now, if you are one of those people who feel they do all of their learning quietly on their own, challenge yourself to read this chapter. Learning is relational whether we are aware of it or not, because interaction helps our thinking. I am asking you to ground your learning in relationships, looking at what others can bring to your search for current knowledge.

Those you select to join you in your journey should be people who bring substantive value to the table through their areas of expertise or particular skills. Those you select must also bring a willingness to be available to you and create the right climate for your thinking and learning. Recruit for your crew the right people —those who will support your learning at all times, even when the weather turns bad or your commitment to riding the current lags. I call them *Practice Partners*.

Learning to ride the current means functioning in a climate of learning, a climate designed to ensure your success in this quest for current knowledge. Let's explore what the right climate looks like (and why).

Thinking Together

As humans we value our ability to think. Yet, we are not as adroit at helping each other think. Perhaps it's because we have always considered thinking a solo activity. After all, it goes on in our heads all the time. But reflect for a moment... Consider the influence of a story told to you that touched you. Remember how much you learned when you discussed a lecture with your study team. Think of how much you discover as you write in the margins of a text (just like a conversation with the author.) Notice what insights you gain when someone asks you questions that draw you out about what you did during the day. It becomes clear that our thinking is really done with and through others. It's done in conversation, in the spaces between the members of the group or community.

In the right kind of community, our thinking can exceed our own expectations of it. Why? Because the right community can actually help us think, encourage us to pursue a line of thought, help us remove hidden assumptions and more. Effective thinking is needed to explore possibilities while maintaining the container that keeps you focused on your learning goals.

Key to the work of this chapter is identifying the person who will serve as your Practice Partner in this work. (If you know several persons you could ask, do so—and consider yourself lucky.)

What should you look for in a Practice Partner? This person's role is to help create and hold for you a climate in which you can think and learn. In this climate, the Practice Partner is willing to listen carefully to your thoughts, ask questions to help you explore them more deeply, encourage outlandish ideas, praise your successes and give you time to finish your sentences.

Moreover, this person is willing to think with you

by listening for the limitations you may be assuming for yourself or the situation, and if not stated, to help you articulate those assumptions. Then, this person helps you explore where your thinking might lead if you were to take the assumption away. Nancy Kline, author of *Time to Think*, calls this question the 'incisive question™' and uses it to great advantage to help her clients think more effectively.

The Right Kind of Thinking

Although we believe that we think in every circumstance, we are right and wrong. For example, it is true that my brain is active when I am driving a car. But if I know the route well, I am more often driving under 'automatic pilot.' I know the trip so well, that I can function effectively while my mind is actively thinking about something else. How many times have I arrived home and not remembered the trip? I bet you've had this experience yourself.

Contrast this to a time when you are chatting with a group, talking about a topic of keen interest to everyone. Your thoughts are moving from one to another with great speed. As one person says something, you find yourself surprised by an unexpected linkage. Then as yet another speaks, you suddenly have a new insight. You ask the group to listen—well, you might even yell, "Wait! I have a great idea." Hopefully, the group welcomes the exclamation and asks to hear more.

This is a different kind of thinking. This is thinking that invites new possibilities to become evident. It is thinking that gains from diversity in a conversation—within the content and among the participants.

Now, how can you create more of this latter kind of thinking as you explore the possibilities your knowledge-seeking produces?

Providing Social Support and a Learning Climate

Just in case you don't quite understand how valuable the right climate is, here is a story about stepping into the climate, rather than trying to create it, in order to help you understand the power of the learning climate in which you are working.

Elaine Peresluha, minister in the Unitarian Church, described many times when she felt she was learning at her best—as a student at the Harvard Divinity School or when parenting her daughter. However, the one that stands out is her trip to Central America. Her original intention was to learn Spanish and have a cultural exchange. Her job was to make deliveries to people in these countries by driving a truck—one among a caravan of 21 trucks doing the same thing. Her task put her in the middle of the cultures with which she wished to have an 'exchange'. "When we got into a community of people who were receiving goods that we were delivering, whether it was in Nicaragua or Guatemala or El Salvador, the stories of these people and their lives so touched me that I was changed forever. I stopped being a U.S. citizen on that trip, and I started being a member of the global community that felt so interconnected. My consciousness of what I consume, what I do, of how my every action has impact. It was a visceral experience that changed me forever." Entering the very space she wished to learn about allowed her to learn so well that she became something new.

Elaine Peresluha wanted to learn about the culture of Central America, and so she placed herself directly into that culture. In her case, creating the right learning climate meant stepping into what she wanted to learn. Her mind had to be focused on the culture around her, and as it did so, she allowed that culture to affect her.

Like Elaine, you will learn from the learning climate you create for yourself. You will actually become more knowledgeable about the **subject** of learning, and how you individually learn best. This enhanced knowledge and self-awareness is a byproduct of learning to ride the current.

A final suggestion for finding the right crew: find people who demonstrate a knack for *Appreciative Inquiry*—whether they are familiar with that term or not. Let me introduce the term with examples from my own journey.

I was named a division chief in the World Bank in 1982. I was surprised that I had been selected a chief after only three years at the Bank and that I was one of only six women selected for management in the entire organization. I was nervous when the time came for my very first performance evaluation as a division chief. There were so many issues that I was trying to address to assure that my division was doing the right things for the department and the institution. As the evaluation began, my manager could not have been clearer. "The memos coming out of your division have too many typos. You have to make sure your administrative assistant's work is perfect." I couldn't believe what I was hearing. (Now, if this doesn't relate to life today, remember that this was in 1982.) The feedback was clear; it was delivered in a pleasant manner, and it didn't help me figure out what I was supposed to *do* as a division chief except make certain that we made no little mistakes.

I went back to my office, called in my administrative assistant, and told her what the director had said. She didn't receive the news very positively, but over the next six months, we worked on creating perfect memos. Across my division, we all hunkered down to make sure that we made no typos. We also made no progress on my vision for the division. Our focus was on typos. It took another six months before we were back on track toward the vision.

Fast forward several years, and I am in conversation with my advisor at the University of Tilburg in The Netherlands. I had decided to pursue a PhD, and I was meeting with my advisor for the first meeting about my writing. His comments were all about what I had done well. He praised the stories, he said that my voice was clear in the writing, and he said the research design was excellent. He never said what needed to be corrected. He only focused on what I had done well. Imagine my reaction to hearing him focus so specifically on what I had done well. I sailed out of his office and back to my writing. I knew what was working and by omission what needed to be changed. But I also knew how to change—enhance the stories, keep my voice, build on the research design. The dissertation flowed out of me so long as I remembered his wonderful encouragement.

We act on what is in our minds. If we focus on a business problem, we tend to lose track of the vision. In my case, the entire division lost six months of work toward our vision as they looked for typos. That's the problem with pointing out problems. If on the other hand we are told what we do well, we are drawn to focus on what is working and how that can be used to accomplish other things. It's just natural to act on what we are thinking. Appreciative inquiry is a philosophy that builds on this natural tendency.

Appreciative Inquiry is a process that engages individuals in organizing their activities around what works, rather than trying to fix what doesn't. It is the opposite of 'problem-solving.' Appreciative inquiry focuses on how to create more of what's already working, and how to evoke the best in people, their organizations, and the relevant world around them. It builds on strengths to achieve the desired result.

Creating the right climate requires the right attitude—a positive state of mind. If we focus on our vision of a positive result, we work to create that possibility, obviating the problems. If we are praised for doing something well, we strive to do it again, better. This change in attitude creates a real shift in both attention and in energy. Following our attention, our energy goes toward the goal. Nothing is wasted on directionless avoidance of the 'non-goal.' Efficiency as well as effectiveness is achieved.

Jackie Kelm, author of *Appreciative Living: The Principles of Appreciative Inquiry in Personal Life* says it well when she speaks of offering an appreciative eye, seeing and focusing on what works, what brings rest, what is of value, what is beautiful. "It suggests we build on our strengths, successes, and best practices to achieve our greatest hopes and dreams."

Using an appreciative approach to build your personal knowledge approach creates a climate that recognizes the direct link between asking a question and creating change. It honors our ability to choose what we explore, and in that choice, to act in a manner that empowers us to achieve our dreams. Your Practice Partner needs to understand this. This is part of offering support and encouragement by seeing what is working and calling attention to it. This doesn't mean not probing for hidden assumptions, but it does mean helping the seeker to see strengths.

You will find that I have structured the questions you will encounter throughout this book using an appreciative manner. They are designed to clarify strengths, interests and successes. Weaknesses are not relevant. Gaps here are considered exciting new territory to explore, not problems to be solved. The appreciative framing of the questions will help you maintain high energy to sustain you as you go. Every task, every exercise I'll ask you to complete is built on appreciative principles.

Find a Practice Partner who is willing to focus on strengths, even while she questions and helps you probe your thinking.

In her research, Barbara Frederickson[6] learned that bringing positive emotions into various learning settings creates a setting where people are more flexible, creative, integrative, open to information and efficient. Negative emotions tend to produce limiting survival responses. Positive emotions trigger energizing/enlivening responses and broaden cognitive ability.

Asking Good Questions

Along with the right climate and a Practice Partner who is willing to think with you, there is a further consideration: The mind works very well against a question. The more specific the question, the better our minds seem to like it. Having someone who will help you think by asking you good questions is valuable.

If I ask an audience at the end of a talk, "Are there any questions?" I get questions. But if I ask my audience at the end of a talk, "How will you use the lessons just presented in your work?" the quality of the comments is several levels deeper and more valuable to the person responding and to the rest of the audience as well. (It's usually more valuable to me, too.) Your Practice Partner should appreciate the value of questions that are specific to help you think more effectively.

To bring great questions into your work of riding the current, consider selecting a Practice Partner who works in a different discipline. Such Practice Partners will ask unexpected questions; even the language they use may be new to you. Assumptions will have a very hard time hiding when viewed from another discipline.

---

[6] Frederickson, B. L., & Branigan, C. (2005) "Positive emotions broaden the scope of attention and thought-action repertoires," *Cognition and Emotion*. 19, 313-332.

Yvette Hyater-Adams describes this in her own way. She is a consultant who works with some of the most complex management issues. As such she feels compelled to be always at the edge. She says, "I need a group of my peers—true peers—who can hold their own, change, challenge, and be challenged, and feel as though they've learned something from the experience... I want to be really stretched in my field, and I'm finding fewer of those opportunities."

Like Yvette Hyater-Adams, you should seek a Practice Partner who can challenge and support you simultaneously while you go about the business of thinking, so that your thinking (and the subsequent learning) goes deeper and explores unexpected places.

Available for Conversation

The Knowledge-Seeker's crew requires avid conversationalists. The right Practice Partner will be curious enough to ask questions, especially from another perspective—and will have the ability and willingness to listen deeply to your answers.

We should all have at least one person we can trust to explore ideas with us—even crazy ideas. I've been lucky. I have found several people (not many, but more than a few) who offer me the kind of relationship where I can explore ideas, problems, and, yes, successes. Although it is fun to call them and tell them about a success, the greatest value of the relationship is when I want their thoughts on something I am struggling with. It's not a matter of whether they agree with me or not. It is all about asking me a question that helps me see my hidden assumptions. Then I can decide if the assumption is real and take the right action. My understanding always improves because of such friends and colleagues.

When I asked people what wishes they would like to have granted that would allow them to remain fresh in their field of knowledge, the most popular response was about being in conversation with other people.

Artist and expert in conflict resolution Dena Hawes' wish is "to have this kind of exchange of ideas. I want to work together in conversation because people bring all kinds of ideas to the table. In conversation, I absorb better!"

Katherine Grace Morris, depth psychologist, sees it as also providing energy. "One of the things I find in working with other people is that sometimes we need a little extra chi, extra energy, and working with others provides that. It's easier doing a mundane chore if we're doing it with somebody whose company we enjoy. That's a key part of learning," she says.

Terrence Gargiulo, author and consultant—and master at metaphor—wishes for a "huge camp fire with beloved people and time to hear their stories and connect with them."

Find a partner who is willing to give you time—willing to be available for conversation.

Let's take a moment to review why a knowledge-seeker needs partners. We've just explored five ways in which a partner provides assistance. I've explained why this assistance is so fundamental to the work of learning that I've developed the concept of the Practice Partner to describe it. To summarize, the Practice Partner you select should be able to:

- Provide social support that keeps you energized about your learning.
- Help create the right climate for your learning to take place.
- Use an appreciative approach designed to direct energy toward what's working well.
- Ask great questions that help you think more

effectively.
* Have time available to participate with you in this work.

Most of the work you and your Practice Partner do will take place in the medium of conversation. What is so magical about conversation as a means for seeking knowledge? Since I'm not there to converse about it with you, you'll have to read on.

Conversation: How We Learn Together

As you might have surmised, I have strong feelings about the integral relationship of conversation to learning. Come with me as I dive into the topic.

Where is Knowledge Born?

For thousands of years, it was believed that knowledge came from on high. Then the Enlightment produced a view of individuals as the creators of knowledge. In the 1970s Social Constructionism emerged, asserting that knowledge is derived from and maintained through social interactions in relationship.

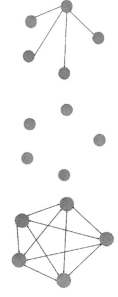

Medieval Perspective: Sees
knowledge coming from on high.

Enlightenment: Sees us as
individuals who all learn and create
knowledge, as distinct from the
theological.

Social Constructionism: Recognizes
that knowledge is created in the
spaces (relationships) between us
through conversation.

For thousands of years, men and women believed that knowledge came from God[6]. It was a one-way flow from the top to the bottom that creates the world and what we know of it. Then there came a time when people realized that they had knowledge in their own heads. They thought new thoughts, came to new realizations, even proved that the new insights were scientifically true. Knowledge could be created in the mind and could change the world. This has been called the Enlightenment. Now, knowledge resided in the minds of people, not just in the mind of God. Around the 1970s, there was an additional insight about where knowledge is gained and its force to change the world. People began to observe that knowledge was gained in the spaces between people through conversation. Even the great thinkers of history were in conversation with others as they thought through their ideas. Galileo wrote to many of his colleagues, including his own daughter, who added to his understanding, even if only through questions. When reading, we are in conversation with the author. New knowledge is the product of our being in relationship with others with whom we converse. And this new knowledge changes the world we live in, even to the point of creating it. This concept (presented here in only the briefest of descriptions) has been called *social constructionism*[7]. Some believe that it will form a revolution of thinking equal to that of the Enlightenment.

Social constructionism focuses on uncovering the ways in which individuals and groups participate in the creation of their perceived social reality. Social constructionists hold that all knowledge, including the most basic common-sense

---

[6] My thoughts here on this subject are guided by Western thinking. I do not claim to understand the greater understanding that includes Eastern thought.

[7] Several references about social constructionism are offered in the Related Resources section under that title.

knowledge of everyday reality, is derived from and maintained through social interactions in relationship. It is a field of study pursued by a community of scholars and practitioners concerned with the social processes essential for the construction of reason, knowledge and human value. Two books on this subject are listed in Recommended Readings at the end of this book. (Some use the term *social constructivism* instead.)

Calling social constructionism a revolution of thinking may seem a bit extreme, but consider the knowledge that is now created as a result of the Internet providing the opportunity for conversation across thousands of people at once. Wikipedia is a prime example. Even blogs offer opportunities for conversation and the creation of new insights. If you are a technologist, consider the expansion of understanding that has come out of Open Source programming. But let's look at an example that is small enough to hold in our hands.

When I go to the theater, I assume that the actors have been given a script that has been memorized, their movements have been choreographed, and they have rehearsed to the point that each action is replicated night after night. I assume that every actor is simply adding his or her piece to the puzzle of the play. Then I began reading Viola Spolin, recognized internationally for her "Theater Games" system of actor training. Her training is about unlocking the individual's capacity for self-expression, but only as a reflection of what is happening with the others on stage.

Imagine improvisation (or even a written play) being performed with the actors simply acting their parts, doing what they want to do, without reflecting what is going on around them. It would be neither improvisation nor a play. It is through the actors' mutual reflection that a meaningful piece is created. Spolin in her work invites the actor to work with the whole space, not independent of it. It is as if the actor is in conversation with all that surrounds him, not just in conversation with the script or himself.

The play of life is not written before we play it. The play of life is written **as** we play it. Actors who do improvisation tell us that the most important thing in improvisation is to listen to the other actors. In life, just as in improvisational acting, we will have the best effect if we remain listening to the voices and actions around us. As we respond, we become a part of creating the meaning, the knowledge, and the world of the next moment.

How can we read Spolin and not say that the space between us is a space richly filled with interaction that brings so much to the world and, more so, creates it? Consider outer space—where we thought it was empty, scientists are finding all manner of matter. So, in our social systems, the spaces between us are filled with creative interaction. Social constructionism is the outcome of this new understanding—an understanding that recognizes knowledge as 'social artifacts' coming from our interaction with each other.

Social constructionism recognizes that we create knowledge in conversation with each other.

Where the Conversation Takes Place

"Two-way conversation provides two-way learning." Claudia L'Amoreaux

In what space does this creative power of conversation work? It can be virtual; it can even be asynchronous (like email or listserves). But many practitioners of this approach speak about their bias for face-to-face conversations, conducted in real time. "I want to have more space for face-to-face conversation. Space that is also playful. When picturing the conversation in face to face, it is fun…I have had to limit the time I spend with colleagues face to face, and I miss it." Claudia L'Amoreaux laments the loss of meeting with her colleagues face to face even as she communicates with hundreds of people across the nation virtually. She tells a story. "At the market, I met a person I had stopped emailing, and she showed up without cell phone or email. We had a wonderful conversation... We need to figure out ways to go off cell-phones and email [and allow ourselves] to just hang out." This was from a woman who has been emailing since 1985 and has seen the gains and losses to this. "I want to create a new way," she says.

Cait Cusack, a medical doctor who works in research, makes real efforts to enhance her ability to stay fresh and on top of things. "I wish there were more opportunities for face-to-face conversation meetings with the people I'm working with because a lot of interaction is through teleconferences or email. I wish there was much more of getting together in one place and making that a priority. I was on a call yesterday where I said, 'Guys, the best way to get this done is to meet together.' And so, that's what we're doing."

Mary Alice Arthur, management consultant extraordinaire, lives in New Zealand. "I learn better with people, so the distance and the cost of travel are real barriers to me. If they were gone, I would keep turning up places!"

Where is that huge camp fire with beloved people and time to hear their stories that Terrence Gargiulo mentioned? We are all longing to be invited to it.

Now is the time to get into conversation with others, be it face to face or some facsimile thereof. Let your colleagues (your ship's crew, to revisit our metaphor) help you develop the learning approach that keeps your knowledge fresh and alive even as you deal with the deluge.

Better Conversations Equal Better Learning

"If I have seen further, it is by standing on the shoulders of giants." Sir Isaac Newton

Conversation always offers an opportunity for learning. Even those who love to learn by reading or by experimentation also learn in conversation with others. The reader is in conversation with the author. The experimenter is in conversation with past and contemporary experimenters, using the language of their shared culture[8]. While each may prefer to be alone with his books or working on her 'experiment,' conversation exists and offers them differing interpretations of what they have read or observed, thus, enhancing learning. Beyond this silent conversation, there remains active conversation with friends and colleagues. Here, the conversation takes on more dynamic aspects. "Conversation doesn't just reshuffle the cards: it creates new cards," writes Theodore Zeldin, in his book, *Conversation: How Talk Can Change Our Lives.*

Mihaly Csikszentmihalyi, a professor specializing in psychology and management with the Drucker School at Claremont Graduate University, says, "Conversation is the core process of shared learning in most work settings and is the starting point to building individual human and organizational capacity simultaneously."[9] This seems to happen in two ways.

First, in conversation, we are able to ask questions directly of others. By doing so the lesson we are learning is reinforced,

---

[8] Csikszentmihalyi would say 'sociocultural context' rather than culture. (Creativity, p. 23)

[9] Tamara Woodbury, "Building Organizational Culture Word by Word" Leader to Leader, Winter 2006, p. 49.

Colleagues in Different Places

It's easy to think of colleagues as only those at work. Yet there are so many other places in life where people, not referred to as 'colleagues,' act as such. Molly Dogget is a high school senior who participates in many activities along with her normal studies, and she has a real appreciation for what it means to have colleagues to work with. One of her extra activities is dance. Again and again, she is faced with a new dance to learn. "I do plenty of group dances. We rely on each other to learn the choreography." Even in the marching band, she says, "We work as a team to learn."

amplified, and embellished by the thoughts of others at the moment of our peak curiosity—something I call a learning moment.

Second, when someone asks a question, the act of responding is also a learning moment. Suppose you ask me a question. As I articulate a response, the concept becomes clearer to me. The very act of formulating a response to an unexpected question can call out previously assumed points. Once articulated, those points are out in the open and enhance understanding. How many times have you answered someone else's questions only to say, "I wish I had recorded my answer. It captured something I have never said before, something I didn't know I knew."

In the organizational context, often the knowledge we are seeking is not written anywhere. When this happens, conversation becomes more and more important. To learn, we need to talk to those who might know the person who knows. And then we need to find that person and talk with him until he is able to understand our specific need and fill it with his experience. We learn in this conversation.

Think back yourself, and you will remember seeing people learn while they are in conversation with others. Even when the conversation is with a dead author, it is still a conversation between the reader and the author's words as each brings an alternative perspective to the topic. When the conversation is alive and dynamic, the learning is richer and more likely to stretch to and beyond the edge of known knowledge. Moreover, it will be more likely to be remembered. The pioneering philosopher and psychologist William James said, "The art of remembering is the art of thinking. When we wish to fix a new thing in... our mind,... our conscious effort should ... connect it with something else already there. The connecting is the thinking; and if we attend to the connection, the connected thing will certainly be likely to remain within recall." [10] Once again, learning is seen as relational – here in terms of relating to what we already know.

Connecting is aided by conversation. Conversation is filled with examples and stories of experiences, and each of these helps us find the connections for our thinking. It is in the interaction, the unexpected question, the new way of phrasing that new insights are gained. Building on the learning that occurs in conversation is paramount to creating a plan for riding the current.

Seek Learning Between the Disciplines

I mentioned earlier that great Practice Partners can be found by looking outside your own discipline. Let me expand on that thought now.

"Innovation occurs in the white spaces between disciplines," said John Seely-Brown. We all come with the assumptions of our disciplines. It is only when we must confront another discipline that our assumptions become clearer to us and vice versa. In my work, I often ask myself to look at a situation

---

[10] William James, (1842-1910) "Talks to Teachers on Psychology: And To Students On Some of Life's Ideals", (1899)

from the discipline of a gardener. Is water called for or should I prune? Suddenly the assumptions I have been holding about the situation are revealed. By looking from another discipline, we open white space, we expose assumptions, and we reveal more areas to explore in our learning.

Conceptual artist Dena Hawes decided to get a PhD in conflict resolution. One of her stories is from the time before learning conflict resolution but reflects the seeds of why she later pursued this different area. She was working in Azerbaijan with an international NGO (nongovernmental organization) that gave money for promising projects in civil society development, private enterprise development, and policy reform.

She was working with the country director who was from the US Department of State. At meetings, they would listen and come back and debrief. What Dena observed at the meetings was completely different from her colleague. Dena says, "We heard and observed totally different things. I see things differently. I'm trained differently. I listen to what is not said, what's half said. I watch body language. I get a sense of the feeling of the room. [My colleague] is taking notes on a more literal approach, on what is being said exactly." But what is said is not all that is said. Dena felt that what was expressed verbally was not necessarily the message of the speaker. She thought the two observations together would be more compelling.

"I watched between words, the pauses, feelings in the room, what's not being said. The nuances are so important to me especially as these were cross-cultural conversations. There is meaning in these, and the literal words can only carry a certain amount of weight." Here was a perfect opportunity for the conversation between two people to enhance the full understanding. Dena's colleague could never understand this. She was focused on the details, and Dena, a conceptual artist, was looking at the whole. Each saw the world from very different perspectives. Imagine the rich conversation that might have ensued as each explained to the other what they had seen and the meaning they ascribed to it. The opportunity missed here will never be fully known, but it was a perfect example of the potential of different voices bringing more to seeing the whole.

Not only is conversation a vehicle for learning, it can be further enhanced by allowing more voices to enter the conversation. Each voice brings another perspective. Seeing the same object from different perspectives is a powerful means of discovering totally new insights. For example, the perspective of the shop floor supervisor is quite different from the division manager. Both are valid and become enriched when shared. Consider interpreting a new policy from headquarters that looks different to the supervisor than to the manager. To understand and learn the policy, imagine how much better it would be if both were in the same conversation as they explored the policy's meaning and how best to apply it. What better way to bring differing perspectives than by adding other people to the conversation.

Communities of Practice (well known to those who are active in Knowledge Management) that are presumably made up of people who are in the same discipline still bring differences—of experience, of background, of preferences, of passions—each of which expands the possibilities of what may be found in the white spaces. People of different minds can expose more and more of that which is hidden to the enhancement (and delight) of the one who is trying to learn.

In this discussion of conversation's role in learning, I've offered you observations of social constructionism and the work of Viola Spolin. I've confessed my yearning, shared by a number of my interview subjects, for more time for face-to-face conversations. I've shown how conversation primes us to learn by allowing us to ask questions that draw out what we want to know, and allowing us to speak what we didn't know we knew. I've invited you to step into the white space between disciplines, where past assumptions become clearer, and new areas reveal themselves for exploration. I hope I've succeeded in motivating you to find an interesting crew to engage in the many stimulating conversations that will occur on your learning journey.

Finding the Right Crew: Moving Forward

In this chapter we've considered the relational nature of learning from several different angles. As you prepare to select your crew and move forward, pause to take in this concept of a *climate for learning*.

Who wants to set out on a journey into bad or unpredictable weather? Motivation is often dulled when the weather turns poor. In selecting the right crew for your journey, you create the climate that will support your learning tasks. You've minimized the risk of 'bad weather' causing a delay or detour as you navigate toward your goal. I hope I've convinced you how important it is to surround yourself with a crew who will help you maintain the right mindset by valuing (and even enjoying) conversation, being willing to ask questions, and giving you room to think through your own understanding in an appreciative manner.

Comparing Accompanier, Practice Partner, and Fellow Seeker

If you've been reading this book's chapters in sequence, you've gotten to know the concepts of the Accompanier and Practice Partner. You've realized that you are the primary seeker of knowledge, and that, for best results, you should surround yourself with other seekers with a similar interest in learning to ride the current.

But I've encouraged you to use this book in a nonlinear fashion, 'launching' where it will be of most value to you. For that reason, I offer Table 3.1, which summarizes the roles and characteristics of your potential crew members. If you have not yet recruited your Accompanier, now is the time to get serious about that step. Suggestions follow the table.

The Crew Member and Role	Characteristics desired in this person
ACCOMPANIER Facilitates accomplishment of the task by providing information and /or contacts	Sees the broader picture in which the seeker lives. Deals well with the mistakes of any learning process. Has shown open-mindedness. Is willing to support you in your efforts. Sees benefit to himself if you succeed.
PRACTICE PARTNER Creates a learning environment of conversation, listening, and questioning, all with an appreciative attitude.	Is a trusted colleague who values the seeker and her desire to stay fresh. Is capable of thinking with curiosity. Has no hierarchical relationship with the individual as a part of this role. Understands that recognizing assumptions are an important part of learning. Gives you time to finish your sentences.
FELLOW SEEKER Is a seeker just like the primary seeker, willing to engage in conversation and think critically and appreciatively.	A trusted colleague who shares the desire to keep fresh by riding the current and is committed to following the process.

Take time now to do the following exercises. These are to help you prepare for the search for the right crew, then take the right actions to gain their support as you embark.

Finding the Right Crew: Preparatory Exercises

Read through the following five questions. Record your answers in your journal.

1. Think of people who make you comfortable to be with. How did they create this comfort?
2. When you have a difficult problem, what kind of person do you go to for help?
3. Is there anyone in your life who always seems to ask just the right question?
4. Who can you always depend on to give you a boost?
5. Is there a group you meet with regularly who might be willing to join you in your quest for keeping your knowledge fresh?

 ## Finding the Right Crew: Action Exercises

Right-of-way rules act to save time and energy (and ultimately, ships and lives). Because the pilot doesn't have to make the decision about which ship passes the other and to what side, he spends his energy on maneuvering the boat instead of making the decision. All the exercises in this book are designed the same way —to help you focus on learning and prevent wasting your time and energy. Moreover, they are designed to ensure that your energy is not frittered away but rather is constantly added to. Wouldn't it be great to travel by a means that ended up with more fuel in the tank than when you left?

First and foremost, keep in mind that looking for what works, your successes, your strengths, will keep you attuned and energized to take action.

Second, you need to decide if you wish to have a Practice Partner. If you don't, go to the third item below. If you do, then you must select and invite the person you choose.

To help you choose, here is what Practice Partners should do for you:

- Listen carefully; ask questions to explore more deeply; encourage outlandish ideas; praise successes; give time to finish sentences.
- Listen for limiting assumptions and help you consider possibilities if the assumption is removed.
- Really know how to ask questions, is curious, demands clarity.
- Be aware of his or her own assumptions (or want to be so).

The Practice Partner both challenges and supports simultaneously.

Three qualities distinguish a good Practice Partner and the relationship between you:

1. There is a level of trust between you and your Practice partner.
2. There is a willingness on the part of the Practice Partner to suspend judgment.
3. The Practice Partner has reason to see you succeed.

It is useful to go over the role and qualities of the effective Practice Partner with the person or persons you invite to do this. In that way, they can know from the start what will help you. They will be able to decide if they will be able to commit to helping you. Be sure to take some time to introduce them to what you are doing and how much time you will need from them. Gain their agreement that what you are asking is reasonable. Lastly, discuss how and when you will want to call upon them and begin the Practice Partner relationship.

Although I have been talking about a Practice Partner who will help you think through matters, best is a Practice Partner who will also be willing to do the process along with you, reversing roles. This makes for a dynamic arrangement where the two of you support each other in both the tasks and the thinking process.

The role of the Practice Partner is not the same as that of the Accompanier. Remember, the Accompanier's job is to support you in your work, not judge it. There are no right or wrong answers. The key is to help you think things through. Ask these questions of yourself before approaching a candidate for the role of Accompanier.

* Do you feel comfortable enough to make a mistake in front of this person? If the answer is yes, then fine. If the answer is no, why have you chosen him in spite of this?
* What evidence have you seen that this person is open-minded?
* What makes you believe this person is interested in understanding what he is hearing and curious to learn more?
* How has this person demonstrated his support of you?
* What benefit will this person gain if you succeed with your plan?

A few of you may choose one person who will play both Practice Partner and Accompanier roles. If this is the case, be aware that the role of Practice Partner is more challenging—to you!

✓ Expected Results/Outcomes

* Decision about a Practice Partner
* Agreement from the Practice Partner (if you have chosen to have one)
* Agreement on how and when you will 'think' together
* Confirmation that your invited Accompanier is ready and able to accompany you with an appreciative approach

 # Record and Reflect

Record in your journal what you learned about yourself as you explored whom you might ask to be a Practice Partner and Accompanier for this work.

Record notes about stories that exemplify these lessons learned.

Figure 3.3: Excerpts from Madelyn's Journal

...Having a Practice Partner is something that would be enormously valuable. Ever since Robert died, I have not had an ongoing Practice Partner, and I am missing this.

...in my career, there are fewer and fewer people who have more experience than I do in my areas of expertise. This is a tricky situation to be in. This is the place where learning is the most critical. It would be so easy for me to say that I have enough to... This doesn't feel right given my own philosophy It opens the door to my becoming stale.

Actions:... First is to ask Barbara to be a Practice Partner who will question everything, yet not be judgmental...

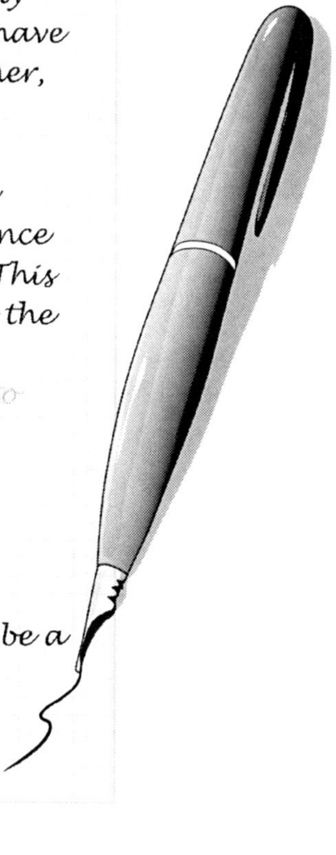

Possible Options

After you've reviewed your work from this chapter, brainstorm a list of people who could serve in the roles of Accompanier, Practice Partner, and Fellow Seekers. Remember, you're not committing to invite each person on the list—you're creating a list of possible options. As you learn to ride the current, your work will be enhanced if you are able to recruit at least one Accompanier, Practice Partner, and Fellow Seeker to serve in your crew.

Review your list, and create your action plan for engaging the crew you'd like to be part of your journey.

Possible Actions: What Others Have Said About Finding the Right Crew

- Seek out those who are expert in your areas of need or simply practice in them
- Seek out and join new communities of practice
- Create a community of practice
- Attend conferences and listen carefully
- Keep looking for ideas, not just perfecting skills
- Call in peers to assist you in your next challenge (offer to be available if they ever call you in, and certainly offer them food)
- Make it a habit to regularly ask the question, "What am I assuming about this?"
- Find a 'thinking partner' and learn together how to be each other's thinking partner (See Nancy Kline's book)

Lessons Learned

In this chapter I've focused on helping you answer the question, Who should you ask to provide social support and to help create the learning climate for your journey? I've given you exercises designed to help you choose individuals with the right characteristics for each role, to increase your success (and theirs) as you proceed.

This is a good time to review your notes on this chapter, and also to review the self-assessment tool presented in Chapter 1. Will you be moving from this chapter to Chapter 4, Stocking Up Supplies for the Journey? If you are not working through the book sequentially, what chapter is right for you to move to next? What have you learned that you would like to record for use in that next step? Write down your observations now.

Optional Advanced Topic: Using Your Network

In the December 2005 *Harvard Business Review* article "How to Build Your Network" by Brian Uzzi and Shannon Dunlap, there is a suggested exercise that can be used to examine your network more carefully. It also offers great insights into what is needed for an effective network. Yes, if you want to do this exercise, you will need to locate a copy of the article. It only seems right to begin your search for new learning by searching! Just to offer a reason to do so, here are some benefits of 'wide networks' as Uzzi and Dunlap describe them. (Wide networks are ones rich in social capital and include powerful brokers who aren't in positions of formal authority.)

Benefits of wide networks:
- They bring in private information (not available in the public domain) that offers otherwise unknown insights.
- They open you to a wide range of skills and diversity of perspectives to help you 'develop more complete, creative, and unbiased views of issues'—important to innovation and learning.
- They are more likely to include brokers who are powerful in connecting otherwise separate clusters of independent specialists, i.e., widen your network further.

As you consider your crew, relate the need to decide whom to include back to Chapter 2's discussion of the need for a container to provide boundaries to your learning. Usually networks of people are not thought of as part of a discussion of containers. Yet, there are ways to assess whether your network includes unconscious boundaries. Read the article by Uzzi and Dunlap to explore this topic.

Whether you choose to recruit a wide network for your crew, or focus on building a team that will work within the container you've chosen with relatively little permeability of its boundaries, is up to you.

Riding the Current

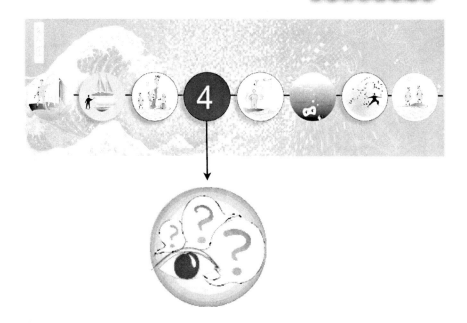

Stocking Supplies for the Journey

"[The perspectives from others] are the grit in the oyster. We argue, disagree, we talk to each other, we play off each other, and I enjoy that proving ground." Howard Milner

Who would depart on a journey without giving thought to the supplies needed along the way? Ships have personnel dedicated to this matter—quartermasters, they are called—and so should you. The metaphor of a ship and its voyage in search of treasure continues to be useful.

In previous chapters I have referred to your quest to deal with the daily deluge of data as a voyage in search of sunken treasure, and named you the captain of the ship. I have

The Accompanier's Role:Participate Fully and Encouragingly

First, help your seeker through participating in conversations. You will likely be included in the interviews suggested in the first preparatory exercise.

Make yourself available for your interview. Answer the questions thoughtfully.

If others who have been asked to be interviewed ask you what is happening (this sometimes happens in a small group,) take time to answer their questions, and be sure to mention the value of the exercise to the person and the organization (if applicable) when the individual has completed his or her plan.

Be curious about what your seeker is learning, but don't exhibit pressure. Inquire about the schedule of interviews. If there are people who are important information sources, you might ask if the seeker has them on her list. To show your ongoing support, ask how things are going. Did the individual get all the interviews she wanted? Needed?

If you are working with your team on this, it might be valuable for the team to make suggestions to one another on whom to interview. As they work together, overlap is likely, and some of the members might have to shoulder more interviews. Doing a little coordination among team members could avoid this and help to widen the field of interviewees. Your voice in this could also be helpful. You know who has worked together and who has good insights into the other members of the team. Helping them take advantage of these facts will enrich the interviews. However, as much as possible, allow individuals to make their own decisions.

Then, as your seeker learns about observation, be very encouraging. The observation exercises are tasks that the individual can do independently. As a result, these tasks may be done cursorily, or may be delayed. The key at this stage is encouragement. Rather than ask why they keep putting off completing those exercises, you might ask what source she placed on her list was the most surprising to her. Note how this question embodies the spirit of Appreciative Inquiry.

Now, if you have initiated this project with your team, it might be appropriate to have a session for the team to discuss their lists together. Remind them this is not a test to see what people use as their sources or who uses the most, but rather to discover new ideas of potential sources they might use. Also, the discussion is likely to remind individuals of sources they already use but have forgotten. The key is to encourage this step. It is likely to appear dull compared to other activities, yet has real value. Help your seekers see that value.

emphasized the importance of choosing the right vessel (the container bounding your knowledge) and the right crew (friends and colleagues in special roles). Now, let us consider other assets necessary for a successful journey. You will need the right supplies —and techniques for using them—to stay nourished as you travel toward mastery of riding the current.

There are two categories of supplies essential to carry with you on this trip: stories and observations, seasoned with perspective. In this chapter we'll first explore how observation brings new insights, then consider how stories help us learn. The common thread connecting these two categories of supplies is *perspective*.

Let me begin with three stories from both my experience and others, to illustrate how important perspective really is.

It was summer, and I was on vacation. My husband and I had gone to a small resort on the Shawangunk Ridge in New York State. Although we spent a great deal of time walking the trails most mornings, that morning I was in a watercolor class. The instructor was teaching how to create horticultural paintings in the English style. She gave each of us a zinnia. Now, a zinnia has a lot of petals. I couldn't imagine myself drawing all those petals and making them look right. So I did something I had never done before. I turned the flower over and decided to paint it from the back, the place where the stem comes into the center of the last and largest row of petals. I spent several hours working on my picture. (Horticultural painting takes time.)

In the end, my watercolor was only fair, but my understanding of the zinnia had taken leaps and bounds. I saw how the stem meets the flower and gives it definition. I saw how the green of the stem was only one of the many colors that are hidden to the casual observer. I was able to appreciate for the first time the gentle convolutions of that last row of petals as they encircle the stem. It was a new experience. Changing my physical perspective, the relationship between my eyes and the flower I was observing, made all the difference.

Elaine Peresluha, a Unitarian minister, understands how gathering perspectives from others expands her understanding of herself.

"The people that I trust most are the people who hold me accountable for what I think is important. If my parishioners tell me something I need to do differently, it touches me at one level. But when my colleagues give me feedback, it's a whole other piece because they know the context in which I work. They have the same credentials and understanding of our profession as I do. Their viewpoints hold a different and more significant weight for me than anyone else's. And I trust that as our relationship over time has built my confidence in them, some more than others. So, relationship and intimacy gives them access to me, knowing me, and knowing where to give me feedback, and where to push me. There is a special power and authority that my colleagues have in my heart." Without her colleagues, Ellen would be missing many important insights.

Conversation is often the medium by which different perspectives come together to create new knowledge.

When I worked at the World Bank, every Tuesday morning my division met to go over problems together. These meetings were gentle free-for-alls where everyone had a chance to contribute, ask questions of each other, explore what the problems meant to their portion of the work. Jason (names have been changed) always looked at the implications to his part of the work. Maura talked about the assumptions that she had made that should have made the problem not a problem. And Sarah just came up with idea after idea and question after question, talking almost nonstop. It was a noisy affair but always friendly. A lot of problems got solved.

Tom, one of the members of the team, usually sat quietly, letting his mind play with the ideas that were being batted around by the others. He sometimes wished that they would just stop talking and let him think—especially if Sarah could just be quiet for a bit. As the discussion went on, he had more and more in his mind that seemed to be coming into focus. When it was in focus, he told the team what he had concluded. He found that usually his idea was received well. Often, the discussion stopped there, a decision was made, and the team moved on to the next item. Tom took pride in his ability to help the team come to a swift conclusion.

One day, Sarah, the most talkative person on the team, the one who always came up with the craziest ideas, was not in. The team began as usual with a discussion of the current problem. But without Sarah, the discussion seemed to falter, and even Tom was unable to help. His mind was certainly working the problem, but he couldn't seem to come up with the same kind of broad-ranging options that he usually did. As he considered this, he realized that he didn't think as well without Sarah's contributions. He had to laugh at himself. We realized that our meetings produced the best discoveries when the interaction of our perspectives was liveliest.

Three stories—the first a very personal one on changing physical perspective and learning new insights; the second reflecting how learning arises from the multiple perspectives present in a community of peers; and the third showing how different perspectives work together to create new knowledge. The common theme is seeing from another vantage point. Powerful learning occurs when we are open to a world that demands a multiplicity of views. Finding different places from which to see yourself and your fields of interest is essential.

This stage of your work will begin with some observations about yourself, then gathering stories through conversations with others, in order to explore where your strengths lie—whether you are aware of them or not. There is much about ourselves that we know we know. Yet there are things we actually know but are not aware we know. Just as others see only a part of us, they may see aspects that we are not aware of ourselves.

We all think we know what we know, but in conversation, we can learn about ourselves things we didn't know before. It happens when others are able to articulate what they see from their perspective. Of course, this has the potential to feel like criticism. You may gain some insight into those areas where you need shoring up. But if you are having the kind of conversations recommended in Chapter 3—conversations that use an appreciative approach to provide a supportive climate for learning —the main focus will be on your strengths.

To explore this concept, take a moment to do the following preparatory exercise. Then I will explain why these conversations can be so fruitful.

Special Preparatory Exercise: Seeing From Another Perspective

Select a common object from your life—a telephone, a computer mouse, a hairbrush, a bowl. Turn the object upside down and observe the differences in appearance from this new perspective. Did you learn anything about the object you didn't know before? If not, you didn't look hard enough. Turn it to a new perspective and look again.

If you are lucky enough to have a baby near by, take some time and watch how the baby deals with a new object that is placed in her hands. Imagine what she is seeing and learning as she explores the object.

Take a moment to record your answers in your journal.

Observation: Keeping an Eye on the Weather

"To shut off observation, we shut off ourselves." Terrence Gargiulo

At the beginning of this chapter, I stated that two categories of supplies are essential aboard the "Knowledge Seeker"—stories (gathered in conversation or reading) and observations (insights gained by shifting perspective). Stories are like food; they nourish the crew, keeping its members fit to perform the operations necessary while the vessel is at sea. Keen observation gathers what is happening at the moment even before it is put into stories. And when you think about all the tools for observation a seagoing craft carries, such as telescopes, sextants, maps, sky charts, and so on, it's clear that observation is an important and ongoing activity aboard ship.

Two of the people I've introduced earlier put it so simply. Elaine Peresluha, the Unitarian minister, said, "I am only as good a minister as I am an observer...If I don't observe and take it in, I don't respond effectively. This is the biggest example of not being current [in my knowledge]."

Creating time and opportunities for observing, and for reflecting on those observations, "makes me smarter" says Claudia L'Amoreaux. Perhaps it's time for you to do some observing, too.

Observation: A Portal to Learning

Whether consciously or unconsciously, when we are observing, we are ready to learn. By observing we've opened the door to transformative thinking, leading to new insights.

Howard Milner is a professional singer and voice coach who is interested in the excellence required to be a part of the professional world. He's deeply curious about the magic that makes music special and why people want to engage in it. He teaches at the Royal Academy and also coaches individuals who wish to use their voices to greater effect.

He says, "You work on the unconscious, and you work on the conscious. To sing, it's about the awakening of the conscious mind to the unconscious process. Music itself lives beyond the self in the unconscious. The whole point is to create a highway to let it out."

Milner believes that every individual is unique, and in his world, everyone has his or her own sound. Tapping into what makes them unique and helping them find their own sound, he knows they will begin to do good work.

In Milner's work, observation plays a major role that is both conscious and unconscious. "It's about observing, hearing, experiencing what your students come up with, working out where they are and then moving them forward with their consent." He goes on to say, "I want people to throw away everything they've learned and then just start again with listening to themselves and letting their own feelings of rightness and wrongness talk."

In the interviews I conducted for this book, the topic of **observation** is more present than any of the other strategies mentioned, when people talked about how they keep their knowledge fresh. Even when done unconsciously, clearly observation is informing the person, keeping him fresh and connected to the situation.

I was particularly impressed with how the politicians talk about observation. County commissioner Jan Gardner said, "When we (Board of County Commissioners) are discussing a topic, I always look at the body language of the people in the audience because they'll tell me when I'm going down the right or wrong path by very subtle body language. And what's interesting is that there are some people that I know what they mean even if I don't really know them because they have such strong body language. Like Chief Dine with the city, I had never met him, but I made eye contact with him and I knew what he was trying to say. It was very strange! He came to me once and said "You had another question on this, didn't you?" So I asked him, and he answered it. ...That's how I use observation all the time."

At the state level, Rick Weldon, member of the Maryland House of Delegates, reversed his position on stem cell research. (He recounts this incident in Chapter 5.) Rick said, "[Observation] is the most important thing...and **self-**

observation was the key component in that stem cell incident. I recognized that intuitively I knew what I didn't know. Politics is a people business. My employers are 40,000 residents of Frederick County. If you don't have [observation] skills, you won't survive. If you don't have the ability to watch and listen to what people do and say, you won't last long in the business, so the power of observation is important."

Milner's comments about observing his students made perfect sense. But the emphasis by the politicians on observation was surprising. They are keenly aware of watching their constituents and needing to do so. No wonder that our federally elected officials get sidetracked when they come to Washington and can see their constituents so much less. The President himself must have the most challenging position. Representing 350 million people makes direct observation virtually impossible.

Eyes Wide Open

In everything that Deb Maher does as a consultant, her eyes are wide open. "I study what's going on in the environment, the way young people are, the good and not so. I look at change in décor, buildings, design, starkness. Is it human/not human, does something lead to interaction or alienation? I always try to figure out what would I do to make this environment more human, and I got that a lot from the urban design training I had in Baltimore, where I learned about urban design and planning and development, and I got to work with some of the best of the best. So looking at the environment and observing how people treat each other… It's about finding commonality to inspire each other."

We all recognize that children learn how to eat, learn how to walk, learn how to talk from watching and listening to the world around them. In the adult world of work, we likewise learn how to behave in an organization from our observations of what works.

This is why we speak of a honeymoon period for the new manager or the trial period for the new employee. Usually it is not to determine if the individual can do the job--it is more to determine if the individual can do the job within the organization. Let's look at an example.

After a reorganization, my division at the World Bank inherited a new staff member. He had come from another division where argumentation was the norm. At our first staff meeting, he joined in with loud, pushy behavior. Our division didn't run that way. If you had something to say, you just said it, and the group explored the options together. Arguing for your position wasn't one of the behaviors for success in the group. I could have let the person learn this in time, but I was more concerned with having him productive. It took only one quiet, private conversation and a week for him to observe and think about the message, and he had adjusted his behavior completely. Without this adjustment in his behavior, he would not have been able to get anything done in the division—a loss for everyone. After the behavior change, everyone enjoyed having him on the team and productivity went back up.

Knowing how to get things done in an organization is powerful. Learning how to get things done comes from observation —from those quiet talks with people who agree to help us 'learn the ropes,' and from putting what we learn into practice, then observing how it works. (When sports metaphors tend to fill our business language, I was excited to be reminded that 'learning the ropes' comes from the days of sailing ships. A sailor had to learn how to tie knots and know which rope hauled up which sail.)

While we are often told that we learn from our mistakes, that statement runs counter to the spirit of Appreciative Inquiry. Approaching the same learning task in an appreciative manner, we learn what to **do** from watching what **works**. In the example from my division at the World Bank, the individual spent time observing how the other members of the division worked together. This was prompted by the quiet conversation we had together. People with a keen ability to observe (and imitate) need fewer of those quiet talks to learn the ropes.

Instruction to "not talk with your mouth full" was a great beginning at good social behaviors at the table, but it isn't quite enough for attending a State Dinner. Your knowledge of what not to do must be accompanied by knowledge about what to do and how to do it. A second chance at a State Dinner doesn't happen often.

We are surrounded by millions of bits of information, and yet, it is important to observe as much as possible and then even more. When we consciously observe, we become more capable of selecting what is important to us, what fits into our container.

Rodger Whipple, owner of a manufacturing plant expands the definition and use of observation still further. "For me, I tend to be a non-verbal person, so I tend to observe and even communicate this way. Some regard this as looking only. I tend to regard observation as hearing, listening, whether they are talking to me or not. It is also seeing because dealing with things that are mechanical becomes sensory observation. For example, I might use my hand to measure the pressure of the air flow, or hold my hand in different ways to see what the air is feeling like. ...So observation is done on multiple levels, multiple senses. For example, at a trade show, I go to engineering, but I am always aware of communication on the markets, sales possibilities, gossip. This leads to insight with regard to where the market and products need to go. This is about keeping on the leading edge."

The Observer Becomes the Observed

Observing others is how most of us get through situations that are new to us, where we need insights into what behavior is acceptable and what isn't. Observing ourselves in action is harder to do.

When we try to observe ourselves, we make assumptions about what others are thinking. We make assumptions about what we bring to the situation. And we often fail to take the time to clarify our own intentions in the action. In a personal learning approach, attention to asking others to observe us begins the process of learning how to observe ourselves.

Try the following preparatory exercise to hone your self-observation skills. The exercise appears simple, but those who have done it find it mind-bending.

 # Preparatory Exercise: Honing Observation

For three days, observe every item you read, every television show you watch, every radio program and podcast you listen to, every web site you visit, every blog you really read, every time you watch someone (including youself) doing something from which you are learning. Just observe and be aware of them.

Simple Observation

I subscribe to nine periodicals, six listserves, and uncounted newsletters come into my mail box. Moreover, I probably order four to six books a month. My office and my inbox are full of them. And at last count, I belong to seven collaborative spaces.

I know it is important to stay up in my fields, I know I should read more, and I know I simply don't have any more hours in a day to handle all that incoming information cover to cover. I decided to begin observing what I was actually reading.

At the top of the list was my daily perusal of the New York Times online in order to keep current with what is happening in the world. Setting a time limit for this obligatory task, I have forced myself to learn how to scan for content instead of reading word for word. Then I noticed that of the nine periodicals, I only opened six of them. The other three land on my 'to be read' pile. I noticed that of the six listserves, I read only two on a regular basis. And as for newsletters—I observed that I regularly tossed ninety percent of them immediately. I found that I always looked at the books when they arrived and did a quick scan of the table of contents, but very seldom read one cover to cover. Of the seven collaborative spaces, I visit 3 of them regularly. The others must ping me before I look at them. At the same time, I realized that I was almost never listening to the podcasts I had subscribed to. Yet, I am always ready for a conversation with a colleague who asks. So many revelations! And all I did was take the time to observe my own patterns.

 ## Creating a Short Inventory: Action Exercise

Using what you learned through your observations in the preparatory exercise, generate lists for each of the following six categories.

1. List the publications you regularly read. Mark the ones that match your areas of strength or areas of interest. Which fall inside the boundaries of your container?
2. List the informative television or radio programs you watch or listen to during the week. Do any of them serve a role in helping you achieve your knowledge goals? Can any of them do so?
3. Check your Internet browser. Is your list of Favorites (Bookmarks) organized? Does it reflect your favorite blogs,

chat rooms, news feeds? Have you recorded them in
something like Del.icio.us where you can locate them more
easily using tags?
4. What groups do you belong to or simply attend regularly,
where you have access to knowledge through other people?
5. Who are those you seek out regularly for their knowledge?
6. What work groups, task forces and committees have you
been a member of in the last two years? In which of them
did you learn?

Record your results in your journal. If you are using a
content management system, this should be simple to organize by
topic.

Stories Nourish Riders of the Current

We create identity and relationship with others through
stories. Consider this Jewish teaching story, which appeared in *The
Story Factor: Inspiration, Influence, and Persuasion through the
Art of Storytelling* by Annette Simmons.

"Truth, naked and cold, had been turned away from every
door in the village. Her nakedness frightened the people. When
Parable found her she was huddled in a corner, shivering and
hungry. Taking pity on her, Parable gathered her up and took her
home. There, she dressed Truth in story, warmed her and sent her
out again. Clothed in story, Truth knocked again at the villagers'
doors and was readily welcomed into the people's houses. They
invited her to eat at their table and warm herself by their fire."

This fable works on at least two levels—it passes on the
wisdom that stories are more readily accepted than 'truth, naked
and cold'—and at the same time, it uses that very wisdom to
deliver its message.

Chapter 3 dealt with choosing the right crew for "the Knowledge Seeker"—the people who surround you on your journey. What is the nature of your relationship with each of your chosen crew? Being able to have good conversations with others is a *sine qua non*[11] of learning. Entering into a deep conversation usually demands a sense of ease with the other members of the conversation. Do you have trust and confidence between you, as Ellen Peresluha the Unitarian minister did with her colleagues?

Do you feel part of a community of peers? If not, you need to get there. So let's see how such relationships can be built, than melded into a vibrant community. Not surprisingly, I find **stories** to be the key.

A community comes alive through telling its stories. Imagine trying to learn about your hometown without someone telling you a story about it. That's why we love pictures from the past that show how the town has changed on the outside. Main Street of the nineteenth century begs to have a story told about it.

When we read the history of a great war, it is never as interesting as when we hear the stories from the lives of the people who lived through it. Ken Burns' series, *The War,* is a perfect example of this. Suddenly, the years between our lives today and the events of the war are foreshortened, and we begin to feel something of the nature of the events. Through their stories, we find common ground with people long dead.

In the same way, by telling the stories from our communities, we begin to feel something of the nature of the community. We begin to find what makes the community what it is. And all organizations are made up of communities. They may

---

[11] *Sine qua non* – without which [there is] nothing; indispensable.

be called units or divisions or teams, but they function as communities. People who work together form communities by building relationships with each other and by creating links between each other, forming a common ground. They accomplish this unity by sharing their stories with each other.

Executives think the common ground is the company's mission statement, but that is only a small part of the beginning. The more viable, real common ground is the stories of the company, one staff member to another (including the executive), one customer to another. At Disney, it might begin with, "Did I tell you about the time when Walt...." The storyteller then tells of a time when Walt did something extraordinarily supportive of creativity. It might be about the time he took an enormous risk to allow something very creative to be born. Walt Disney created a culture that valued creativity—a value of Disney to this day. The stories about creativity don't end with stories about Walt either. Stories about the high social rank of 'imagineers' (the folks at Disney who create the rides at the theme parks among other things) reinforce this culture of creativity. Culture is formed by the stories that are told and retold within the group of connected individuals— an organization, a team, a society.

Paul Costello, founder of the Center for Narrative Studies, creator of Living Stories™ and the Narrative Room™, guides individuals and groups to create new stories to inform and form renewed communities. Costello begins almost every talk he gives on narrative with the phrase, "We are born into stories from before we were born." And the audience rediscovers it again and again. The first maxim of Costello's work on communities and story is: "We recognize that we are born into language before we are born into life. Language both precedes us and outlives us as both ecosystem and 'echo-system.'"[12]

Our identity is wrapped in our stories. Many of us were named after an ancestor. That person's story becomes part of what parents tell us about the name and why we were given it—just one of the stories from before we were born, that anchor us in the community we call family.

We often introduce ourselves by telling others a story about our family, our life, our work, our selves. The listeners begin to

Early Words

When growing up, I remember my father telling me again and again, "To thine own self be true." (Excerpt from Polonius' long soliloquy to his son, Laertes, "This above all: To thine own self be true, for it must follow, as the night the day, thou canst not then be false to any man," from *Hamlet* by Shakespeare.) It became part of a daily story he told us. I never knew the other words from that famous soliloquy until I had grown and gone on to college, but it was too late by then. The world I lived in required me to be true to myself. What always confounded me was the surprise on my father's face when he saw his children doing amazing things as they lived into the story of being true to themselves. He had created a world for us that he didn't imagine.

form an image of who we are.

Stories are neutral in and of themselves. Each story presents a series of events of one experience, from one perspective. As I listen to your story I can disagree with your conclusions, but I can't disagree that the story represents the way you experienced

---

[12] Costello, P. "Recovering Collective Memory: Toward a Narrative Method of Cultural Healing." Storytelling Magazine, January 2002

the series of events. It's the neutrality of a story that allows it to enter into our consideration, and so begins the process of communicating who we are to others.

Moreover, telling stories to one another offers a potent means to establish and grow relationships. We form relationships with those who have a similarity to us whether that similarity is about values, intentions, capabilities or interests. We need to find common ground on which a relationship can stand. Story identifies the possibilities for common ground and provides the planks for building a bridge to it. Once the relationship is formed, we can expand the possibilities and the common ground. As the common ground grows, we feel safer and safer with the relationship and ultimately with ourselves. That feeling of safety exemplifies the right climate to encourage learning.

Stories Provide the Context of Learning

Stories have a power of their own, which lies in the link between the teller and the listener. As listeners we create our own links between the story being told and what it means to us. When a story is told well (and some would say more simply, if it is told — well or poorly), we react. The moment can be so intense that the listener actually experiences the story — learning lessons from the experience, just as the teller did (but perhaps different lessons, given their different perspectives).

Stories must have a setting, a time, a place, characters, the dilemma, and the resolution. You can't understand the resolution without the dilemma or the dilemma without the characters and setting. In other words, the story carries the context for understanding - for learning. The context is essential to learning. As a result, we can even learn from our own stories.

Learning is done in context, and stories provide context. Case studies have been popular for years, because they are the story of a problem. Today, we realize that the story doesn't have to be about a problem. Success stories, winning stories, transformation stories, future stories—all have the power to teach, because the lessons are enhanced through the context of the story.

To summarize—stories nourish strong relationships, in each of these ways:
- Stories create identity and build relationships necessary to sustain the conversation.
- Stories teach through context.

Story is one of the foundational concepts of my approach to keeping knowledge fresh and alive.

Discovering Your Stories: A Portal to Learning

Now let's connect what we've been discussing about **story** to the importance of **conversation**. In chapter 3, I shared my observations about the integral relationship of conversation to learning, and introduced the concept of social constructionism.

Narrative practice and social constructionism are related. Social constructionism articulates what is happening within the creative space of the conversation and recognizes the power of narrative. Just as the space between us is populated with our language and relationships, our stories do more than identify us. Stories build relationships that enlarge and reinforce the creative space. Stories carry content that feeds our thinking. Stories convey context that broadens the possibility of new insights.

The approach of this book is rich with opportunities for interaction. The opportunities are built into many of the steps, to reinforce the value of learning through interaction with others. As you practice this approach, you'll grow in skill at learning through conversation. This approach harnesses the creative power of the conversation that narrative practice and social constructionism offer us.

I am about to invite you to some of the most dynamic conversations of your life. I will ask you to interview people around you, in search of new perspectives. As you explore what others say in response to your questions, listen carefully to the stories they tell you. In those stories you'll find new knowledge about your areas of interest—and perhaps most important, new insights into what you already bring to the table.

 ## Preparatory Exercise: The Fun of Gathering Stories

When we ask others for an example, we are asking them to tell us a story. This exercise is to practice the skills needed to really draw the story out rather than just getting facts and opinions. In other words, developing your listening ear.

Do this exercise with a friend. Ask him to tell you about a time when he was having great fun. As you listen to him tell you this, write down every word he says that piques your curiosity. When he is finished, ask about every one of those words—to expand on the word for you. What's the story behind it? After he has answered any question you have about the words, see if you can see the whole picture in what he was telling you. Now, tell him the same story as if you were he. You don't have to tell it in his words. In fact, it is more fun if you use your own words. When you have finished, ask him for his reaction to your version of the story. You'll be surprised and have fun, too.

Stocking Up: First Action Exercises

"In every person, regardless of first appearances, there is something to be learned if you remain open." -Kat Pearl, teacher

It's time for you to practice what I've been preaching. Time to engage in conversation, to gather insights from friends, colleagues, your Accompanier and yourself. This exercise asks you to interview eight people. I know this sounds like a lot, but these interviews can be done over as long a period as you wish to give it. So, you might interview three people and continue on with your planning for riding the current. Later, you may feel it is time to interview another and see how it fits into your ride. There are those who continue to interview others simply because it gives them a chance to talk at another level with colleagues.

As you decide the people you would like to interview, consider two points. First, ask people who know you and/or your work, because they interact with you regularly. Second, ask people who will be willing to respond to you as openly as possible. Keeping *Appreciative Inquiry* in mind (as discussed in Chapter 3), I've designed the questions to be fully appreciative in nature. They do not test friendships; they are designed to explore the possible, the workable, the valuable. So, they will provide you useful information and bring energy into the process.

Moreover, people usually feel free to respond truthfully to these kinds of questions. But it is still important to consider if the person will be willing to think through the questions and respond fully. If you feel that someone you are interviewing is not doing so, thank him for his time, and find someone else. If he is telling you things you don't want to hear, but appears to be offering those thoughts honestly, then the speaker probably has some important information for you. The real question to ask yourself is if this person is answering you willingly and fully. If so, you are getting good and useful feedback.

1. Interview three friends or colleagues outside of your work.

Ask for a half hour of time with each of three friends or professional colleagues, and find a place where you are likely not to be disturbed. Explain what you are trying to do and ask this individual to be honest in her responses to you. Tell her that the information is just for you and won't be shared by you with anyone else. (This is a real contract with the person and should be honored by you. If you say that you won't share what she says, keep your promise.) Confirm that your interviewee is clear about what you are doing. Then, ask your questions.

- Tell me about a time when you decided to come to me for information, knowledge or know-how. What was the topic? Are there other topics that you feel I know?
- Tell me about a time when you came to me for help because you felt I knew something that would be helpful to you.

Tell the individual to take her time. Encourage her to tell you stories about these times so that you can see the context in which they happened. And when you don't understand or want more information, ask for it. When the conversation slows, ask your interviewee if she has anything to add. To conclude the interview, thank her for her time and insights.

Interview at least three people even if you must spread these interviews over time.

You may choose to record the interviews—or not. After each interview, write up your notes—or not, as you prefer. But do take a moment and write in your journal the points you learned from each interview. For your note-taking, you may have decided to use a spiral bound journal, a notebook, a computer program, a blog, or some other tool. Use whatever works for you. As I've said, if you prefer to write by hand, I recommend a bound notebook of some sort that keeps your notes in sequential order.

2. Interview three colleagues with whom you work.

If you work in an organization, choose three colleagues familiar with your work. If you work alone, challenge yourself to think of three individuals with whom you have worked in the past, or who know your work.

As with the first interviews, ask for a half hour of time with each of your work colleagues, and find a place where you are likely not to be disturbed. As described previously, explain what you are trying to do and ask for honesty in responses. Confirm that the conversation will be confidential, and that each interviewee is clear about your intent. Then begin asking your questions.

- When I am contributing most to our work, what do I do that is of highest value?
- What do I contribute that helps best to achieve what we are trying to do here?
- What information can you always depend on me to provide?

Remind each individual to be thoughtful, as the information is very important to you. When you don't understand or want more information, ask for it. When the conversation slows, ask your interviewee if he has anything to add. To conclude the interview, thank him for his time and insights.

Interview at least three work colleagues even if you must spread these interviews over time. However, there is much to gained by doing these interviews closer together.

Again, after each interview, record the details as you prefer, then take a moment to write in your journal the points you learned from each interview.

3. Interview one person who evaluates your work.

In most cases it will be clear who this interviewee should be. If you do not have a formal supervisor, boss or manager, this is the time to think about who does play that role informally. For example, the independent consultant may choose to talk with a client. If you are a carpenter, you may choose to talk with a master carpenter who is familiar with your work. If you are a politician, you may choose a constituent. If you are a student, you may choose to talk with one of your instructors. Even if this work is entirely for you and your personal goals, be prepared to explain what you are doing when you ask this person for an interview.

Others who have done this activity report the conversation with their manager was one of the most significant ones they ever had with that person. The questions delve into topics often glossed over in normal conversation about the work including evaluation or assessment conversations. So, if you are concerned about doing this activity, don't be.

Ask for a half hour of time, and find a place where your conversation is not likely to be disturbed. It may be in your interviewee's office or the coffee shop on the corner. Explain what you are trying to do and ask him to be honest in his responses to you. Tell him that the information is just for you and won't be shared—and keep that promise. Remind the individual that this work you are doing is your design to achieve your own professional development, to keep your knowledge fresh.   You are doing it on your time, because it is that important to you. Begin by confirming that he is clear about what you are doing, explain in more detail if necessary, then begin to ask your questions.

- Tell me about a time when you felt that I was most successful in what I was trying to do for (whatever brought you together—e.g. your organization, the class, a work project).
- Tell me about a time when I was able to meet a challenge, resolve a difficult situation, or solve a problem.
- Tell me about a time (or times) when you noticed that I shared my knowledge with others.

After the interview, write up the details as you prefer. Be sure to take a moment to write in your journal the points you learned from this interview.

4. Interview your Accompanier.

If your chosen Accompanier is not the same as the person you interviewed who evaluates your work, it would be helpful to interview your chosen Accompanier now. As the Accompanier should be aware of you and your work, use the same questions you posed to the evaluator.

Ask for a half hour of time, and find a place where your conversation is not likely to be disturbed. State that you seek honest responses. Explain what you are trying to do—pursue your professional development by learning how to keep your knowledge fresh. Begin by confirming that she understands your goal and motivation. Explain in more detail if necessary. Tell her that the information won't be shared. Then begin to ask your questions.

- Tell me about a time when you felt that I was most successful in what I was trying to do.
- Tell me about a time when I was able to meet a challenge, resolve a difficult situation, or solve a problem.
- Tell me about a time (or times) when you noticed that I shared my knowledge with others.

Be sure to take a moment and record the points you learned from this interview.

At the conclusion of this chapter, you'll refer back to your journal entries made as part of this interview exercise.

Some of you may never have formally interviewed another person. To help you, I've provided further instructions; see "Conducting the Interviews" in Annex 1 in the Appendix.

✓ Expected Results/Outcomes

In this chapter I've covered two topics; conversation/stories and observation/insights, which I see as connected by their fundamental concern with perspective. If you have completed the exercises related to each topic, you should now have a few (or many) notes to review. The interviews have given you practical experience at using the techniques discussed in this chapter.

Record and Reflect

For each of the interviews you conducted in the preparatory exercise on conversation, you should have insights gained through your interviewees' responses to your questions. If you have written about the interviews in your notes in detail, highlighting the insights you gained during each will help you become more aware of what you are hearing.

Record in your journal the list of insights you have gained. You don't need to record all of the insights from all of the interviews. Pull out the most important to remember as you prepare to move to the next step. Don't shortchange yourself. Take time to reflect on what insights you have gained and which are most important to you. Don't be surprised if you discover that you have gained more insights as you reflect on the individual interview insights you listed earlier.

You should also have new insights garnered from the exercises on self-observation. In your journal, write down the major themes that arose for you. Write them in full sentences. Highlight the most important lessons to you.

Figure 4.2: Excerpts from Madelyn's Journal

...I turned over a heart shaped piece of sculpture in amber that has sat on my desk for years. When I turned it over, I saw a much... I saw it was concave. No wonder the piece always feels so good in the palm of my hand.

Lessons from the interviews:
I was most surprised by the observation from one individual who said that I constantly look at the world as if I had never seen it before. That I select carefully what I say to others. And while I may accumulate information, I share specific...

Actions:
I must find a way to bring my verbal abilities more naturally (easily) into my writing...

Possible Options

Review your notes and insights, and create a list of possible options for action to stock up for your journey with stories and observations. Write possible action steps that will get you using observation to learn what works well and how to do it—and how to observe yourself more accurately and thoughtfully. (This is an appreciative way of continuing the search.)

Possible Actions: What Others Have Said About Stocking Supplies for the Journey

- Suggest that your team select a time when all members will come together and have an informal coffee (with pastries!)
- Reduce the number of publications you receive and try to read
- Increase the number of publications you receive and read
- Identify courses, workshops, or conferences that focus on your areas of need
- Join List Serves that regularly post items of interest
- Read article summaries and select only valuable articles to read in total.
- Maintain a database of valuable articles that are tagged or have key words attached to them along with the location of the article.
- Seek out discussion spaces on the Internet that are relevant and take time to determine if they are worth regular visits or occasional check-ins
- Review your 'bookmarks' or 'favorites' and trim them down to those that really are useful (or organize them to speed up your searching)
- Create a book group to spread the reading load
- Join Del.icio.us and begin tagging sites for easy return

Lessons Learned

Review your notes on this chapter. Perhaps take a moment to review the self-assessment tool presented in Chapter 1. Will you be moving from this chapter to Chapter 5, Equipping for the Dive? If you are not working through the book sequentially, what chapter is right for you to move to next? What have you learned that you would like to record for use in that next step? Write down your observations now.

Riding the Current

Equipping for the Dive

"I find learning enormously difficult because it involves acknowledging how wrong I've got stuff, and the better I get, the 'wronger' it gets." Howard Milner

I never realized how much one could learn from beginners until I listened to Terrence Gargiulo, who coaches fencing for the Junior Olympics in his spare time. One day he was watching the swimmers and realized that a master coach was just observing a beginner coach teaching a beginner student. Terrence asked him why he was doing that. The master coach responded, "I can learn more from the beginners. It is almost Zen-like. It is the feeling." Terrence reports that he learned something that day, too.

The learning moments in this short story are numerous— observing the swimmers; observing the master coach reflecting on the scene, asking a question, and allowing the response to sink deep into him.

The Accompanier's Role: Prepare to Learn

The results of this step will feed the creation of a customized learning approach for the person you are accompanying. How a person learns best is individualistic. There is no right or wrong way to learn, but each of us has developed approaches that we find more effective for ourselves. The key task of this chapter for the seeker is to find new ideas about ways to learn, and to explore which she is drawn to and which she might typically resist.

While any good learning event includes many forms of conveying the lessons—presentation, discussion, experimentation, quiet reflection and more—when a person understands how she learns best, she is better prepared for learning through any format. Why? Because she recognizes her resistance to learning something she wishes to master may simply be a reaction to the style in which it is being presented. Perhaps that style is simply not her preference. Once understood as a resistance within herself to the form of presentation, she can choose to open up to the lesson rather than remain in resistant mode.

Thus, for you as an Accompanier, an unexpected outcome of this step will be the insights you will gain about how you can convey information to this person in the future—and to others. For example, if this person finds experience his preferred way to learn, you can use case stories to allow him to 'experience' the information through story. If you are this person's manager, you might offer him an assignment he has never done before and assign it to him with a partner who has. If he prefers to reflect on things before moving forward with action from the lesson, consider ways in which you can aid him to do this reflection. For example, you might ask him to make a presentation to the rest of the team to explain a new concept. This will force him to reflect on what he has learned in order to present it to others.

If this is a project for your team, you have other options. Although the task is individual in nature, a team discussion of the results will provide stimuli to each that will prompt new ideas as well as reminders of existing sources. Moreover, this discussion can help the team in its work together. If the team agrees to share their individual insights, they will learn a lot about themselves as a team and how to work together better. Working and learning are related.

Learning is complex and occurs through so many means. It's time to explore—how do you learn best?

If you want to dive into learning, you'll need strategies to thrive deep in the 'water' of new knowledge, just as a scuba diver needs equipment, training, and knowledge of the undersea environment. After all, riding the current sometimes means a deep dive after special treasures—in this case, the treasure of learning techniques matched to your own personality and strengths.

The treasure we are diving for is knowledge. But the treasure is not truly ours until we have learned it—really internalized it, made it part of the supplies we carry, accessible whenever we need it.

There is currently a great deal of theory that attempts to explain the different ways adults learn. But theory is not important to you—what matters is simply understanding for yourself how you learn best. This can come from considering how others learn, and seeing how their techniques fit you.

In this chapter I will let the people who spoke to me

speak to you. Among their comments you will find many strategies and, I hope, at least one that particularly speaks to you. If none immediately seems to fit, you will have a chance to try on different approaches until you find for yourself how you learn best. Don't worry; this isn't a test. How we learn is never right or wrong, nor does it need to fit into any theory.

Field Notes From Diverse Divers After Knowledge

I asked each of the people I interviewed to describe one of their best learning experiences. Those interviewed offered some wonderful strategies and stories. As you read these, note the ones that really speak to you.

Learn By Teaching

Ralph Scorza, a leading scientist, is serious about continual knowledge-seeking. When asked about his learning experiences, he told me, "I learn two things: concepts and facts. Facts I can learn just by quick reading. Concepts are more critical to me. First, I want a person-to-person demonstration or discussion—someone to explain from A to B. In this way, I can ask questions. It allows me to get the whole concept. Then I must explain the concept to someone else. Here is where I really learn whether I understand or not. Once I can explain it, I can go anywhere from there."

I was impressed with Ralph's story. I loved the honesty it showed in recognizing that he didn't always learn the concept immediately. How many of us know this deep down, but don't take the extra step that Ralph tells of—explaining to another person. I found myself relating a great deal to his point that explaining something to someone else is an effective way to gauge how much you really understand.

Then I came across another way of using this technique to learn.

Sheila McNamee, Professor of Communication at the University of New Hampshire, uses an innovative approach for testing students' knowledge acquisition. She says, "If you do not wish to take the exam, all you have to do is explain what you have learned to someone else in my office. You may choose the person but remember that he is allowed to ask any question he wishes to help him understand what you are saying. Also, he can't be someone who already knows the subject, nor can he just nod and say he understands. You actually have to teach this person what you know." What an imaginative way to take advantage of a powerful learning technique. Now, this is a useful kind of 'exam.'

In earlier chapters I've spoken of Claudia L'Amoreaux, learning coach. To my question on learning experiences she responded, "When I was studying Maturana, I found it compelling, but very hard to fathom and communicate. I felt passionate to communicate it. I felt frustrated because I couldn't do that well. So, I decided to teach the material. I set up workshops, set up deadlines by which I would have to read and be prepared to teach. I was very disciplined as a result—about reading, about the way I took notes. This helped me to improve how the material came to me and, thus, to others. I used index cards, boxes, colored pens—made it more graphical so I could see the concepts. It was exhilarating to be engaged at that level! It's something I want more of."

So, you see, you can use this technique in at least two ways —Learning by teaching helps you absorb what you are learning, and tests how well you have absorbed it.

Learn By Doing

"My best learning is being able to touch it, feel it, do it myself," said Thomas Deakins, who excels at doing things right. "I am thinking back to the military and the different jobs I had, from running a tank to being a platoon leader. I sat down with the guy I was going to replace and talked about the people and the equipment. Explored what was different. I was doing an exercise in Germany and still a tank platoon leader. I had some free time and I went over and got into one of the trucks of the support platoon, talked to some of the soldiers who were a part of support about what they did. Before, I never got the concept. I need fuel – the fuel is there. I need bullets – the bullets are there. I didn't realize there was this whole other logistics train that I was now going to be in charge of. I talked with soldiers, got the basic concepts. But to actually do it—this is where I learned, learned the challenges, and learned how to make it successful."

Pedro Catarino is a cardiac surgeon in the National Health Service in London. Catarino had been learning for three to four years to operate with the heart/lung machine. "I wanted to move away from this machine. And while my boss did use the machines a lot, he allowed me to try some cases. He allowed me to test myself out in this situation. I knew he was observing and would have stepped in if absolutely necessary. He allowed my learning to take place." Learning this was essential and through the doing brought significant value to the lesson.

Learn By Researching and Writing

Kai Hagen, who serves as a County Commissioner in Frederick, Maryland, is still known for how well he prepares his background materials for decisions. "It is characteristic of me to exhaustively research things. Back in the 1980s I wanted to find a book, and I couldn't find it. So I wrote it. It was the *Guide to the Natural History of Natural Areas of the Region* (Minnesota). I had to visit all the sites. I had to talk to a lot of people... It ended up a 288 page published book. It got good reviews, sold nine or ten thousand copies. I worked very hard to do a lot of research."

Daniel Dixon, a former advertising executive and now in his 80's, continues his early career experience in writing. When I interviewed him, he was writing a book on the ukulele. "I did profiles of people and have a natural interest in what they have to say and feel, and I enjoy that kind of writing – where readers learn about a subject as the writer learns... As I have learned about the ukulele in order to write this book, I discovered a very deep emotional and almost evangelical feeling about the ukulele. I continue to discover things – some absurd, some poetic." In all, his learning has never ceased.

Learning in Conversation

"I think my best learning was when I was accepted in a national program at Neighborhood Reinvestment Corporation," said Deb Maher, who today is a senior consultant to many organizations. "[The program] trained you to become an executive director of a non-profit local public/private partnership dealing with revitalization in distressed neighborhoods... That was a high learning time because it put me in conversation with all kinds of people and all kinds of places, and I was called on to find out information and to communicate it back to them. I was a synapse, I was a connector." Those who work with Deb would agree, she continues to function as a synapse and connector!

Marsha Scorza, who excels in inviting possibilities within conversations, identified a course in miracles group as a positive learning experience. "[In these groups] there are people with similar perspectives but new information, and an expansive frame of reference where the discussion is full of lots of possibilities. We share experiences, expand on concepts; I can ask questions and all give their 'take'. No big ego."

If you've read my earlier chapters, it will come as no surprise that I believe conversation is absolutely fundamental to learning.

Who Helps You Learn in Conversation

If learning in conversation resonates with you, take a moment to think about the kinds of people you like to converse with. Are they people who try to draw the best out of you as we explored in appreciative inquiry where the focus is on building on strengths? If so, you have created a good learning environment.

Or are they people who always agree with you? If so, are they asking probing questions so that you learn by digging deeper into yourself? This is what a strong Practice Partner is able to do.

Or are they people who are always telling stories? If so, you will have a rich set of examples with the context to allow you to learn at two levels.

Are they people from other disciplines who tend to see the world from their perspective, thus enriching your ability to see from a different perspective?

Learning to learn in conversation might be a key element in your approach to riding the current.

Learning Through Curiosity

"I buy books, but I also like to go to places where I can talk with the author, such as in a lecture," said Wayne Salamon, a computer specialist who loves exploring new subject areas. "You can also go to the author's web page and see more, and find podcasts and videos, too. I have a side interest in biology and evolution. Evolution theory is built on a rigorous mathematical basis. The computational models are able to mimic some of the theories. You can even download the models and interact with them, thus, enhancing absorption. But I do like a good book! As I read, I search on the web to explore what I am interested in learning more about. The point here is that by expanding beyond your field, you can learn how others approach information management. Many fields, such as biology, space science, physics, have huge amounts of information." Wayne uses his curiosity to draw learning from the white spaces between disciplines.

When a New Story is Called For—A Must Read

Rick Weldon, Maryland State Representative, was courageous enough to change his position on an extremely controversial issue.

"The most painful lesson I've had in public service deals with the question of stem-cell research. For the first two years of my service as a delegate, I actively opposed it. I actually led the parliamentary work of the Republican caucus to kill the embryonic stem cell research bill, and we were very effective…but there was always a nagging doubt in my mind that what I was doing, I was doing for the wrong reason.

"In August of that year, I went to Delaware, where my parents live, to attend a picnic for my dad's birthday. He and my sister were talking about their diabetes and how it had affected their lives. My dad's could be attributed to bad eating habits and lifestyle, but my sister's was juvenile diabetes. While sitting and shooting the breeze at the barbecue, it dawned on me that the people who argue in favor of embryonic research say that one of the key factors is the potential to create a treatment path for people with diabetes. At this point, I knew I had to find out more.

"I came back here, and I called the stem cell research lab at Johns Hopkins University. I asked if I could spend a day with the scientists.

"I said I've read a lot and been influenced by filters and experiences to make me think a certain way, and there is fundamental and important knowledge I'm lacking. There were questions I wanted answered, most importantly the concept of life and our respect for life as it leads to scientific research. They agreed and made a whole day available. Mid-morning, the head of the lab said, 'Let me show you something. You may not be comfortable with it, but it's important to understand the factual basis of the argument. We have embryos that have been donated to be stored cryogenically. When they exceed storage life or the donors no longer wish to pay for storage, this is what happens.' And he took a test tube and poured the contents down the sink.

"Those are embryos under Maryland law that scientists at the University of Maryland would use to look at potential cures for Alzheimers, spinal cord defects, diabetes.

"Five minutes at the sink—that was my epiphany moment. I became a co-sponsor of the embryonic stem cell bill in 2005 that allows use of those embryos, scheduled to be destroyed, for research purposes.

"I learned so much that day."

Deep learning often requires brushing aside our assumptions. Only then is there room for a new perspective to be considered. Rick Weldon had the courage to set aside his assumptions in order to discover a new perspective. In his case, he changed his operating assumptions. Changing operating assumptions doesn't always happen, but a deeper understanding has no chance of happening without a willingness to open ourselves to the possibility. We must challenge ourselves, as Rick Weldon did, to realize when we need to know more—to find a newer, truer story for ourselves.

Learning Through High Motivation/Need

Rodger Whipple, executive and owner of XericWeb Drying Systems, told me, "I learn most in a disaster. Throughout my engineering career, when I have something not working right, the customer won't take the product, it is not working as expected, we have to identify the source of the problem including real needs and expectations of the customer. This challenges us to examine understandings, assumptions, and beliefs." Rodger is on a constant lookout for solutions to his customers' needs, even without a disaster.

Learning Through Two Media at Once

Jan Gardner, Frederick County Commissioner from 1998 to today as the President of the Frederick County Commission, said, "I always read and write at the same time, or I write and listen at the same time. If I'm doing public comment, I always write what people are saying. Even if I never go back and look at it, this helps me remember it." Jan sits through an amazing number of long meetings just listening to constituents. Efficient learning is a critical success factor for Jan who has been reelected two times.

Learning Through Reflection

"In the evening after a day's work, I sit down with my notebook and take an hour or an hour and a half every night, and just write down, not everything, but the stuff that somehow I felt worked and try to figure out why that worked." Christopher Heimann, director and playwright, uses a consistent reflection time to explore what he is learning about his work.

David Drake is a consultant who helps others reflect on their lives. "I was reading a book by Sam Keen called *Learning to Fly*... It came at a time of great transition in my life. I had met Sam before as a seminary student when I was twenty-four, and now thirty years later, it became a reflection of my whole life. I could look at where I have pulled in, where I have risked in my life. It gave a perspective on my life."

Learning in the White Spaces

We've talked about learning in the white spaces between disciplines. Sometimes, we don't even know the boundaries of our learning. We step into a white space where we learn about learning as well as the topic at hand.

Katherine Grace Morris, consultant and coach, stretches herself every day to learn more. When I asked her about learning experiences, she replied, "Actually, I'm learning something new right now—I'm studying Hebrew. And you know, it requires a different mindset. It's not additive, like the bulk of my learning now. I have a schema for feng shui, for depth psychology, for the gross domestic product. I have a knowledge base in these areas. But Hebrew? I'm coming to it virginally. I have to learn it from scratch with no reference at all. I take classes and I study on my own. I'm finding that I'm doing it how I learned my ABC's when I was a wee little one. One of my textbooks is the sort of book that a kid would use in learning Hebrew…mi ma mo ma mi ma ba ba… going through it letter by letter, just so I imprint this stuff in my head. That's been a real new learning challenge, just a pure learning play." Katherine's new language requires a new mindset —she's not just mastering a new language, but learning a new way of learning – or perhaps using one of her strategies from childhood.

If learning by walking in the white spaces appeals to you, consider the people who walk with you. Do they bring the inspiration of cross-disciplinary thinking? In earlier chapters I have talked about the Accompanier and Practice Partners as two roles your companions might play in your learning process. I suggested that a Practice Partner drawn from another discipline might bring unexpected insights to your process. If

Katherine Grace Morris is finding a new way of learning in her pursuit of the Hebrew language, how much more might she discover if she involved a Practice Partner in her language practice? Consider involving your Accompanier or Practice Partner to help you learn by walking with you in the white spaces.

More Learning Strategies

In earlier chapters, I introduced you to others of my interview subjects. Raymond Douherty is a master carpenter who learned through repetition of iterative experiments with wood, getting to know his materials. Dena Hawes is an artist who made art objects before going to graduate school, where she discovered her love of writing. For her, the decision to go back to school opened the door to learning a whole new aspect of her talent. Bob Sadler spoke of the 'magic hours' he spent in workshops, learning facilitation and collaboration. The workshops gave him experience that helped him put together the puzzle pieces of his own knowledge in a new framework.

If you have taken the time to read the stories of some of the people I interviewed, you have seen that learning occurs in many ways. This is one of the reasons good instructors use many different forms of exercises and experiences within a single class. This assures that the learning preferences of different people are met at least some of the time. Moreover, it's the reason why conferences can be such a bore even when the topic holds great interest for you. Lectures are hard to take for a long period of time, even with slides to focus on. The key here is that we learn in unexpected ways. Always depending on a class to learn something may actually be your least useful approach to learning. These stories show that there are many options for gaining new knowledge.

Learning the Harder Way Can Bring Added Benefits

In the process of developing your learning approach, you have an opportunity to experience many methods of learning. Practicing multiple learning techniques helps to establish the 'practice' of learning.

Once you have discovered how you learn best, don't rest. What starts out as an effective technique can become a straightjacket to your learning over time. For those of us who just love getting into a good book, learning tends to take on the character of reading more and more. Those who prefer to talk to someone who knows the subject will tend to resist long reading. Whatever, your preferences for learning—reading, finding the expert, talking it over with a friend, writing about a subject, playing around with a computer application rather than reading the manual—developing a solid learning approach should include some actions that fall outside your favorite strategies.

Because of your different learning preferences, some of you will struggle with some of the activities in this book. For example, those who find it hard to talk to others may find the interviews you are asked to do scary. Learning using a means that is not your favorite doesn't mean that you won't learn. With practice, you may find you learn more when you try different approaches, because you are more conscious of your learning. (Read Dena Hawes' wonderful learning story about graduate school, if you haven't already. You'll find it in Chapter 1.)

About Practice, Letting Go and Time

I have decided to learn how to do ballroom dancing. It's not part of my professional learning approach, but it is part of my personal one.

At first I learned the steps quickly and easily. My body seemed to almost know them before I learned them. Then came the cha-cha. The basic steps were so easy to learn, right up until the instructor added 'form and style.' When I tried to do it in the class, I found myself trying to think of four things at one time—where my feet were, where my hips were, how to turn and how to make emphasis on some of the steps. I got more and more confused. When I left, I knew I had to practice this or I would never learn it. Well, the week turned into one of those that didn't allow for any free time. As a result, I came the next week with no practice, having forgotten the step altogether. I couldn't even remember the name of the step.

I asked the instructor to show it to me one more time. After he did so, I found that I could execute the step perfectly the very first time—and with all the style and form that he had been trying to teach me the week before. I was amazed. Having set the problem aside for a week, somehow, my body had figured it out on its own. Letting go was the answer.

It is likely that learning ballroom dancing will not be a part of your plan for gathering fresh knowledge. However, the technique I discovered might be. I learned that times of actively seeking out new knowledge and insights needs to be balanced with times of complete letting go and rest.

Of course, the old saying that the more you practice, the better you get, is also true. That is certainly true for your golf swing or driving on a freeway or giving a performance evaluation —or ballroom dancing. But the subtler meaning of practice is to give your mind and body time to learn together. This requires letting go of the conscious search for new understanding at times of confusion, and letting your body and mind do its silent work of integrating through its own form of play.

Exploring How You Learn and Use Knowledge

"The human mind, once stretched by a new idea, never regains its original dimensions." — Oliver Wendell Holmes

One of the reasons my learning approach begins with interviews of other people is to teach you the behaviors needed when exploring the unknown with another person. As you become more adroit at interviewing, you are learning a behavior that will support continuous learning from anyone. In a way it is like dancing because your body and mind must work together in order to accomplish it. You may begin with steps, but soon you are working on style and form.

Learning is an iterative process. Learning one thing entices one to learn the next. The more one learns, the more it is necessary to revisit what has been learned so that it can be tested again, refined, expanded upon, connected to other knowledge. Imagine pushing a circle out from the inside. You push on one side a bit, then move around and push on another side. Slowly you move around the circle, enlarging as you go bit by bit. Then you realize that you have been at this spot before, and so on. Never are you learning the same thing over again, rather you are learning in the same place at another level — deeper, wider. Revisiting a step may feel redundant, but it is not. When a question is asked a second time, the answer always provides more. Deep learning is never a single event.

 ## Learning About Your Learning: Preparatory Exercises

I've given you the observations of many of my interview subjects about their preferred ways of learning, and a glimpse into my own learning preferences. Now it's time for you to learn about **your** learning. Select one of the following exercises.

Exercise 1: Reread the learning stories in the first part of this chapter. As you read each one, note how well you resonate with the story. When you find one that resonates with you, identify what you saw in the story that touched you. Write your observations in your journal.

Exercise 2: Select two or three activities from the following list and do them. The purpose is to sharpen your observations of yourself in learning mode.

- Visit a museum.
- Participate in a dance class, exercise class, or swim class.
- Ask a child to describe to you how they learned how to tie their shoes or color a picture or play a new computer game.
- Play a new game where you must learn the rules before playing it.
- Attend a concert.
- Assemble a model.
- Study a new language.
- Play a new computer game with no help from anyone else.
- Go to a lecture on a topic new to you.

After you have done two or three of these activities, write down in your journal what it was like for you as you did them. Did it feel familiar or new? What was a pleasure? What felt difficult? What was exhilarating? What was a real drag? What surprised you?

Regardless of which exercise you decided to do, consider how the selection of the exercise alone teaches you about your own learning style.

Learning New Knowledge: Action Exercises

This set of exercises can be done alone, but you may wish to find a partner who will help you explore these questions. A Practice Partner is great for helping you be clear about things, for helping you tackle what you would like to avoid as too hard, for helping you see limiting assumptions and for asking you questions that pull out new insights you didn't know you had yourself. (See Chapter 3 for more on thinking with a Practice Partner.)

Some of you may feel that you know your best learning style. You may have taken a test that scored your learning style. These kinds of testing techniques can be very valuable. But we all change over time, and you might discover that you have expanded your style since the last time. Try at least one of the following exercises.

Exercise 1: Set aside some time—as much or as little as you wish —and find a place where you won't be disturbed. Keep your notebook or computer handy so that you can record your thoughts as well as think them. We all think we will remember what we think, but in this case, the task of recording will serve to sharpen your thinking as well as record what you have learned.

These are such important questions you may find it helpful to have a friend ask them of you. Ask someone to put the questions to you, and to keep pushing you to be as specific as possible in your answers. If you already have a Practice Partner, this is the perfect person to help you with this exercise. If not, this is a time when your significant other might be of help. Or find a 'thinking partner'[13] if you haven't already got one.

- Think of a time when you were able to **learn** something new, and you were able to learn it very rapidly and well. What was it about that time that seemed to make it different from other learning events? Who was involved? What was the setting? What was it about the situation that encouraged learning? Why did you decide to participate in this learning? Can you tell a story about that time? Be as specific as you can.

Now gather from this story what seems to be the means that helped make that learning experience so effective. Continue to explore other learning experiences this way until you stop gaining new insights into your best learning approach.

Write up what you have just learned about your own learning. Use at least a half page to record the lessons you just learned.

Now move to the second set of questions:

- Think of times when you had to **find new information**, and you were able to do so successfully. List all the methods you used that were successful for you. Next to each method on your list, note the situations in which you found yourself at the time you used the method.
- What seems to be the motivating factor of what you learn? Are you learning because you feel inspired for one reason or another? Are you learning because you are just so curious? Are you expending the energy to learn because learning alone gives you great pleasure? Consider your answers about these specific learning

---

[13] Nancy Kline has written a wonderful book, *Time to Think: Listening to Ignite the Human Mind* (Warlock, 1999). It presents both the rationale and the process for thinking and how a partner in this process can lead to extraordinary results.

experiences. How does what you were learning fit into the boundaries you've defined, as discussed in Chapter 2? Is it time to revisit the boundaries you have set? (Don't be afraid to do so as you learn more about your own desire and means of learning.)

What insights do you gain from reflecting on my questions? Write those insights down in your journal.

For those who want to take this to the ultimate, here's one more question.

- Take a moment to think of a time when you found learning very difficult. What was it about that time that seemed to make it different from other learning events? Who was involved? What was it about the situation that made the learning difficult? **What did you do that allowed you to learn even in the midst of the difficulty?** Why did you decide to participate in that learning anyway? Can you tell a story about this? Be as specific as you can.

Again, write down your insights and don't be surprised if you learn something valuable about this latter learning event even though it felt hard at the time.

✓ Expected Results/Outcomes

Written insights in your journal reflecting on each set of questions about your ways of learning.

 ## Record and Reflect

Record in your journal the lessons you have learned about how you learn. Write about what you need to do to make learning effective for you.

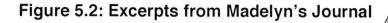

Figure 5.2: Excerpts from Madelyn's Journal

Preparatory exercises: The exercise I chose to do was, "What seems to be the motivating factor of what you learn?" This was a great meditation for me. It becomes clearer and clearer that I gravitate toward things about which I am curious. An enticing article will send me to Amazon.com to find a book and Wikipedia to...

Lessons: I need to want to learn in order for me to learn at all

Possible Options

After you've reviewed your work from this chapter, record notes about stories that exemplify these lessons learned. Review your notes, then brainstorm a list of possible actions to experiment with different learning approaches that fit your preferences, or push you beyond your comfort zone if your preferred style is starting to fit like a straightjacket.

Possible Actions: What Others Have Said About Equipping for the Dive

- Learn to 'speed read'
- Learn to 'trash[14] read'
- Select the most important sources both for general world-view and specific to topic and stick to them at least until you decide they are sufficient or too many
- Give up watching television and focus on gathering from important sources
- Place all notes from meetings (non-project specific) and phone calls into a bound notebook noting date and participants for easy reference.
- Select a computer application that will allow you to organize content (content manager) that is of value to you and is already in your possession or to be obtained
- Hire a reader who is adept at summarizing
- Explore blogs carefully and follow only one or two that really give you value
- Browse through bookstores – really browse
- Check out Amazon's to be published list
- Create a book club so that reading can be shared among you
- Volunteer to be a mentor for a young person (learning is part of teaching, too)
- Insist on conducting AARs (After Action Reviews) after every major activity of a project
- Set aside a day each week for reading either together or spread out over the days

---

[14] [14] Trash reading is anything but trashy. It is a focused search of a book by reading the forward, the introduction, and the table of contents. Then selecting carefully which chapter(s) looks most interesting and reading it. At this point, you decide whether to continue to read the book, more selections, or put it on your shelf with the knowledge that you understand the author's main message.

Lessons Learned

In this chapter I've focused on helping you discover insights about how you learn, to better customize the many possible learning approaches to suit your preferred style. I hope I've convinced you to try different approaches to serve your desire to keep your knowledge fresh and alive.

This is a good time to review the self-assessment tool presented in Chapter 1. Where will your study of riding the current take you next? Will you be moving from this chapter to Chapter 6, Deciding to Dive Deep? If you are not working through the book sequentially, what chapter appeals to you next? What have you learned that you would like to record for use in that next step? Write down your observations now.

Optional Advanced Topic: Creating New Knowledge

Everyone comes up with new ideas at times. The exact strategy depends on the person and the situation. The seeker after new knowledge may have no awareness of the strategy being used; she may be simply following an old habit, early training, or instinct. We all learn through different means, and all can be effective, for certain people in certain situations. In this chapter we've looked at a wide variety of individual preference in learning strategies. I hope you've acquired insights into your own learning approach, and identified some new strategies to try.

If you feel this optional topic is just too much at the moment, skip on to the next chapter. My approach is designed to support iterative learning. If you choose to pass by this exercise today, perhaps you will come back to it when you revisit your notes and insights, to glean more from your study of keeping knowledge fresh and alive. If you decide to try these exercises now, congratulations.

New insights gained through your own reflection are part of staying fresh and alive. So, in this optional advanced topic, I ask you to explore the times when you have created new insights, new ideas—new knowledge. This section pushes you to think about your own thinking process and about the times when you have exceeded your own expectations.

Robert and I loved to work together. We each had different talents to bring the client. I am adroit at helping teams remain on task, staying with the task until it is completed. Robert 's skill lay

The Accompanier's Role: Get Out of the Way

This is an optional topic. If done by the individual, your role is to be responsive to any questions or requests for support.

If this person is open to sharing, ask her to share the situation she chose to consider. Take time to offer your insights gained about your own ways of being creative. This is an opportunity for you to learn how to help this person be more creative. By sharing your own story, you help her learn how to help you be more creative, too.

On the other hand, if you've assigned this project to your team, this is a golden opportunity for them and you. If you need to innovate, you need creative thinking in your team! This is a powerful exercise for your team to work together to discover ways in which each member can help the others be more creative.

Ask the team if they would like to explore their insights together. If they do, then allow them to help each other explore the questions and discuss their answers. Their discussion will identify ways for helping each other be more creative together. Participate with them if they welcome you. In addition to their own stories, suggest they write a story about when the team is most creative. Suggest that they imagine themselves a year in the future, having become this more creative team, as they write their story. Have fun!

in helping teams come up with the wildest ideas. Granted some of them would never work, but then again, some really looked good or with a little tweaking could be made to work even in a bureaucracy. Together, we made a balanced team for getting results that were new and fresh. Wanting to know how Robert did his magic, our client, the manager of the group we were working with, slipped quietly into the back of the room and just watched.

Robert began by doing some incredibly silly things from tripping over the power cord to wearing something backwards as if by accident. The group was laughing before they had hardly warmed their seats. Then Robert asked them to each tell a partner a story about a success they had had in their work — just a short story, but one that would describe something about that success that the partner could use to introduce them to the rest of the group. Even though they all knew each other, the stories revealed new things about each person. One was successful because she was persistent. Another was successful by always challenging himself to be his best. The list went on and on, and the group felt more and more comfortable with each other as they saw the qualities that had led each of them to be successful. By the time Robert asked them to work on the problem at hand, they fell into it as if it was the simplest thing in the world. Eased by laughter and strengthened by seeing their own qualities, that's when the magic began to happen and ideas flowed like water.

The manager could hardly believe her eyes. What had looked like nonsense and wasted time at the beginning had fueled a remarkably creative session.

It takes great courage and self-confidence to open a business meeting by making fun of yourself, yet Robert was one of those people who was more concerned that the group do its best work than being seen as the perfect guru. He knew the environment that would create the right conditions for thinking clearly and imaginatively. In the end, he always drew out the very best from a group.

So often our work, our thinking, our learning is limited by concerns about how we are perceived, how new ideas threaten existing thinking, how we wish to be 'safe' rather than creative. Yet new insights are confounded in such an environment. If you are seeking to remain fresh in your knowledge, you must take time to allow new thinking, new ideas, even conflicting thoughts to come forward. Let's take a moment to see if you can find those times when you have stepped into creative space.

Creating New Knowledge: Preparatory Exercises

Here are two exercises designed to get you into creative space. Pick one of them. The first one is fun and remarkably illuminating. The second is more serious, because it brings in an existing problem from your world. It also takes more time and resources. Pick the one that appeals the most to you.

Turning the world upside down. If I were to ask you what kind of restaurant has no waiters, you would immediately say something like, "A fast food place." If I were to ask what kind of restaurant has no tables, you might say, "A lunch truck on a city street." Now I will ask you think of as many ways as you can think to design a restaurant that doesn't sell food.[15] (It's actually more fun to do this exercise with someone else to help spark ideas. When I use this with groups, they have come up with a great number of ideas. Sorry, no hints allowed.)

Leverage Perspectives. This exercise can take some time if the problem you choose to consider is a serious one. In any event, it requires a real problem. After reading the instructions, you

---

[15] These exercises are adapted from Edward DeBono.

may want to take a few minutes to decide which problem you want to work with — serious or simple — the choice is yours.

Select an existing problem from your work or from wherever you are passionately engaged. Just make sure the problem is real so that when questions come up, there is a context in which real answers can be given. Find five other people to do this with you. Ask each of them to assume one of the following roles as you discuss the possible solutions to the problem. Set a time limit for the conversation (30 minutes is probably the minimum), make certain everyone understands that his job is to listen when someone else is talking as well as contribute to the conversation. Keep contributions fairly short so that the emphasis is on stimulating new ideas, not developing the details of one. Then let the fun begin.

- Person one: looks at the assumptions behind what others are saying.
- Person two: looks at only the cost of an idea.
- Person three: looks at all the reasons why the idea won't work.
- Person four: looks at why the idea will work.
- Person five: looks at the implications of each idea.
- Person six: just comes up with ideas, no matter how crazy.

The key to this exercise is to see what one person says about an idea that stimulates a new idea. This exercise is one that should be done in a fun manner while respecting each role and giving each person adequate air time. After awhile, you can trade roles. It helps to let the juices flow by initially allowing those with ideas and comments to just move along. If some of the roles have not been heard from, pause and make sure they have time to enter the conversation. You want to hear from everyone. Keep track of the conversation. After all, this is your problem, and you may find a startling solution among the ideas offered.

Creating New Knowledge: Action Exercises

This exercise is best done with another person—your Practice Partner if you have one. If you haven't chosen a Practice Partner, find a friend or colleague to help you by asking the questions and pushing to help you be as specific as possible. This is a time when your significant other might be of help. Or find a 'thinking partner.'[16]

Some problems defy prediction. Some problems are so complex, there is no simple answer or solution. Some problems, called wicked problems, have so many variables that they can't be held in a single head. Some problems just demand creativity. Here are several sets of questions to consider. Read through all of them and pick the one that most resonates with you.

- Think of a time when you saw yourself or someone else come up with a brilliant solution 'out of the blue.' What was happening? Who was there? What was unusual about the situation that may have helped this to occur? What time did it occur? Was it a group activity or some other situation?

- Have you ever looked at a problem from a new perspective and suddenly seen a solution? What was it about that time that helped you see that new perspective? Was it a convincing argument? Was it new evidence that you simply didn't expect? What was it?

- Watch a young child deal with something totally new. How does the child approach it? What is different about how he

---

[16] See Chapter 3 about Nancy Kline's book *Time to Think*.

or she deals with a new thing and the way you do? What can you learn from this?

- When do you feel least in control of the information that is coming to you? What is it about these situations that distracts you? Disinterests you? Detracts from your goals?

Once you have explored one of the sets of questions, take time to write a story (yes, a story) of when you think most creatively—and be creative! It may be an imaginary story, but let it show the kinds of insights you have just gained in how you are creative. You might consider the start as "Once upon a time,..."

 # Expected Results/Outcomes

A story about when you think most creatively.

 # Record and Reflect

In your journal, write down the major lessons learned from these exercises. Write them in full sentences. Highlight the most important lessons to you. Return to your notes on *Possible Options* and *Lessons Learned,* and add your new insights to your notes there.

Figure 5.3 Excerpts from Madelyn's Journal

..so how to get people to get to this place in less than a minute. I invented an electronic postcard that contained only three things. First, was a quotation that caught their eye. Second, was a provocative question that helped them think about what the quotation was saying to them. Third, was a simple reference to my company. Ashraf listened. But what could I call this? I told Ashraf about my idea and said that I was going to call it The Inflection Point. Ashraf just listened. It made sense to me, but no one I talked to really got excited about the name. Ashraf was not buying it either and finally he spoke. He saw a different metaphor for carrying my message to the potential reader - one that built on the common trend toward coffee. "You want to juice them up. Right?" "Sure," I said. "Then call it Mental Espresso!*" And so I did.

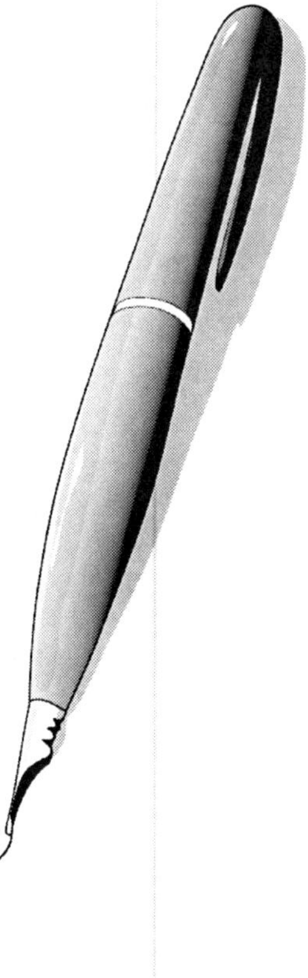

My lesson: If I want to get out of a logjam, I should talk to someone with the ability to think and articulate even the craziest idea. And as I talk to them, I must be ready to tell as much of my situation, my dilemma, my idea as I can so that I feed them with information and time to let their mind play. Then I must sit back and listen.

Riding the Current

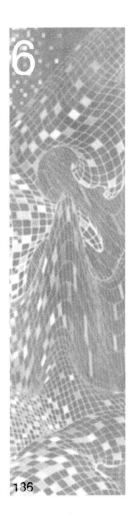

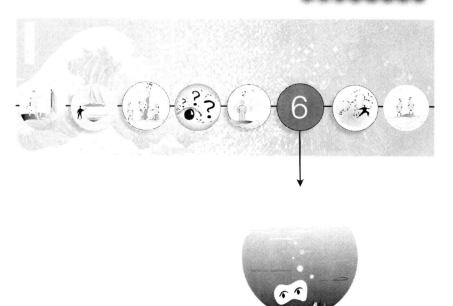

Deciding to Dive Deep

"Never lose a holy curiosity." - Albert Einstein

Some people just do things differently. Peter Block is an author and consultant whose work is about empowerment, stewardship, accountability, and community. Reading his books, I felt I was conversing with a man of great insight. His warm heart and informed mind delighted me. My desire to interview him for this book was immediate. His response was also immediate.

You may have read one of his seven books, including *Community: The Structure of Belonging, The Answer to How is Yes: Acting on What Matters* and *Flawless Consulting: A Guide to Getting Your Expertise Used.* Or you may have come across one of his numerous articles, essays, forewords and interviews. If you have, I imagine you share my interest in finding out

187

The Accompanier's Role: Give Time

This is a time of personal reflection for the individual seeking a new learning approach. You need play no role in it. Yet, this is a step that requires thinking, and this can take some time. Be curious about what your seeker is doing; is thinking taking place, or procrastination? Make yourself available for conversation. Your offer to help your seeker think out loud could be just what's needed.

If you have been working with your team on this, support that by allowing sufficient time for this step. The team members may decide to do some of this in conversation with each other. This is a wonderful team-building activity, but it must be one that arises spontaneously from their process. If the team members have decided to use Practice Partners, then this is a significant place for Practice Partners to work together.

As the Accompanier, monitor your behavior to be sure you are supporting, not leading, this process. Each seeker must do his or her own work of discovering the overall lessons and planning a future in which the lessons learned are assimilated into an efficient and effective learning approach.

what he knows about keeping knowledge fresh and alive.

Riding the current has two purposes for Peter Block. One is the constant search for ideas that are interesting. Peter says, "If you want to change your thinking, seek outside your field. I mostly read people outside my field in every discipline, whether it is philosophy or architecture or theater or poetry." The other purpose is self-development. He goes on to say, "Keep working on yourself. So much of the work is staying ahead of your own consciousness, your own thinking. Thinking matters, which is a radical thought in this culture."

I loved the impression Peter's words gave me, of someone pushing out beyond himself yet at the same time, bringing along all that is himself. There must be a great force that compels this kind of work. "What pulls me are the complexity, struggle, and suffering in the world," says Peter. "It's a complicated world. As I get older, it becomes less and less bearable and captures more of my attention. In the early days, you are worried about whether you will survive. Now, I find it is so hard to make a difference, to do anything meaningful, that matters, that is durable, that goes beyond the surface."

Searching for interesting ideas constantly pulls Peter in new directions. "I change the venue I pursue every six or seven years," he says. "You are not really starting over, you are staying engaged." Peter's strategy is about taking who you are and how you think into a new domain. Peter draws upon feeling and intuition, questions, attractions to find the next area to pursue. But in the end, "It doesn't matter what path. I like the edge. I like the margin—not in terms of risk, but in terms of curiosity. And I think it serves me well."

With such an attitude, Peter often finds himself facing ambiguity. "Ambiguity is a word that captures life as experienced, not as it's talked about. I expect ambiguity. Nobody lives with it happily, but I do think that what is ambiguous is what is interesting about life." If nothing is ambiguous about a movie, it is not interesting and people leave. When it is ambiguous, our attention is captured and held until the ambiguity is resolved. Ambiguity is inherently interesting and allows the holder to reap the potential of great new understanding. Peter has made a cause of seeking the interesting inside of ambiguity.

Peter uses three strategies for riding the current. He

reads a lot—across many disciplines. "When I hear of a book, I really go after it. I get it the same day and look at it and try to absorb it." He pushes himself into unfamiliar places. "I say yes to most invitations. So, I am dragged into places I would not choose to go into, that are awkward and unfamiliar, but force me to pay attention." And he talks about things he doesn't understand. "People ask me to give talks on the books I have written. Instead, I talk about what I want to talk about." Peter's words show me he prefers to share his current interests than to repeat past insights. He's a real master of riding the current, and as a result, his work is always fresh and alive. His approach has made him a highly sought-after thought leader across multiple fields. His strategy almost belies the idea of a plan for riding the current. And yet, his approach is highly successful.

Peter's approach is about following a set of values, not planning specific actions. As he says, "When I feel I am drowning, I dive." For those who are ready for the plunge, the treasure is amazing. Peter Block has found treasure after treasure as he comfortably holds what others would consider to be conflicting ideas. In his hands, ambiguity is offered acceptance, and conflict is made to offer up its secrets.

Working (or Playing) With Ambiguity

Throughout this book, you have been asked to write up the lessons and insights you are taking away from the activities you have been doing. Now is the time to explore them all together and discover the lessons inside the lessons. Don't let ambiguity or conflict stop you.

In Chapter 5, I presented a number of different strategies for taking a dive after the treasure of new knowledge, drawn from my many interviews. In previous chapters, I tried to equip you for the journey, with observations and exercises about how to create the container for your learning, who to take along and how to make the most of their fresh perspectives. I asked you to study your own learning behaviors, to find techniques that help you retain and use the knowledge you find. My goal all along has been to make you effective and efficient as a continuous seeker of knowledge.

All this training as an adult, just to recapture an ability that comes naturally to very small children!

Small children play continuously while at the same time they engage in some of the most challenging learning they will ever encounter. They must learn to move their bodies in a coordinated fashion. They must learn how to distinguish words, syntax, and meaning from a myriad of sounds around them. They must learn where their bodies begin and end. They must learn how to limit the amount of stimulation they receive from their senses so that they can make sense of their surroundings—attending to the most important while ignoring the standard, unchanging stimuli. They must learn the actions that are needed to survive in the family. The list goes on and on, and yet we think of their lives as one long play session.

Adults seem to believe that play is something you do only to relax and recuperate from work or studying. We rarely think of work or study as having any play in them. I doubt we ever recapture the feeling of being an infant again—the feeling of existing in a totally bewildering world and letting it all happen until the mind can sort it out. But there are small moments in our adult lives that look something like this.

Have you ever struggled while listening to someone with a strong accent? When this happens to me, I can struggle to understand every word, and I quickly become exhausted. But if I consciously relax as I listen, so that the sounds just wash over me, I find that very quickly I begin to know the sense of the words, and then the words themselves become clear.

Have you ever gone to a Shakespearean play only to find that you are not understanding the English? Those not expert in Elizabethan English sometimes find it hard to follow Shakespeare's language. Again, if you relax as you listen, just letting it wash over you for a while, you may suddenly realize that you understand it all. It's not work at all when it is done this way.

Then there are the times when two 'realities' seem to be in conflict. I remember being asked what my strengths were and responding with a list of what I had heard others say I was able to do well. Consider my surprise when my questioner said that she saw them not as strengths but as weaknesses. It was ambiguous. It was confusing. Which was true—either? Both? As we have seen in the story of Peter Block, this kind of conflict is a rich one for those seeking to keep their knowledge fresh and alive. I learned a great deal that day and even later as I pondered how my strengths could act as weaknesses in different situations.

Bob Sadler Lives With Ambiguity

"I am an emergent property coming out of a chaotic life!" Those are the words of Bob Sadler, executive coach. " I see everything as ambiguous. I'm not black and white in any sense. I have soft and confused boundaries, which are both a danger and an asset. I have opinions, but no judgmental ideologies as a result. For example, I was coaching an executive who saw himself as great. Now, I didn't see him as 'great' or 'not great,' because I know good and bad can exist in the same situation or person. It may seem ambiguous, but it's possible when you don't come with an ideology or judgmental perspective. [For this executive] I saw it all and said what I saw. I cringe at myself, but somehow he understood that I was not judging, just saying what I saw from an authentic place." Bob Sadler is most effective in his work. He lives in the present with all of its ambiguity and confusion and messiness. "I never let fear of making a living get in the way of what has to be done," he says, and then he lives with the consequences.

More Stories About Ambiguity

Bob Sadler is comfortable in the white spaces between disciplines, between good and bad, between future and past, in the midst of paradox, and has made it his home—to great success.

My understanding of ambiguity in the organizational settings was finally confirmed when I listened to Prusak. Larry Prusak, management consultant and author of *Working Knowledge*, says he must deal with conflicting facts all the time. He says, "Generally, they are both true. There is not much certainty in organizational life. Context is all important. You must remain open and keep a certain distance." He says he is supported by Walt Whitman's line "I am large, I contain multitudes."

Yvette Hyater-Adams, an African American woman, CEO of Renaissance Muse, consults on complex management issues. She says, "Ambiguous situations are major. I deal with apparently conflicting options every day when I look at diversity, because my answer to that is that both are true. There's a term I use, 'frame of reference.' I can look at a situation that looks one way from one side of the street, and one way from the other side of the street. And when you're standing on two different sides of the street, you have two different frames of reference. I don't keep myself in an 'either/or' world. Because when I find myself trying to hang on to either/or places, that's where I get stuck."

"I deal with ambiguity by accepting that this is a 'both/and' world. And that means that you may have to make certain choices in one situation and other choices in a similar situation—and that doesn't mean that you are inconsistent. It's just that you have [to be able to say] 'This is why I did it. It was at this place and time...' For example, people ask about my greatest mistake. Now I really don't tend to think of things as a mistake. I don't know if that's arrogant, but I think of it as if you didn't know something, and it didn't turn out the way you wanted. Then you got clear about what you wanted. So if that gave you an indication that you don't want to do that one again, I don't see that as a mistake."

Yvette's story comes from years of helping others understand that there are usually at least two sides to any story when you are dealing with diversity—or not! What may look like ambiguity can be just perspective, or 'frames of reference' in Yvette's words. Ignorance plays a part, and so, too, does being willing to step to another side of the street.

To help you get in touch with a time when you were in an ambiguous situation, consider a time when you joined an organization that was completely new to you. How did you feel at the first meeting? Perhaps the vocabulary seemed to be a foreign language, because the people were using their words differently from any use you knew? How did you learn to collaborate here? Perhaps you struggled to understand whom to include in a strategy meeting and whom it would be inappropriate to invite. How did you learn how to write for this new organization? Was it in the same style as your former setting? How did you discover the way people in this organization invited you to lunch? Did you recognize it the first time? The list goes on and on.

My first few weeks at the World Bank were amazing. I was confronted with a culture that did not resemble anything I had ever encountered before. It was called multi-cultural, because the staff came from over one hundred countries. They all spoke English, but with a myriad of accents. And sometimes the words didn't mean what they had always meant to me. Since when have people been referred to as 'fungible[17]?' The style of working didn't emphasize timeliness, yet there was an enormous amount of work being done

---

[17] Fungible means designated goods that substitute for any unit of it, such as grain.

very quickly. The offices seemed messy to me (especially as I was coming from IBM when it was still 'Big Blue'), yet final reports had to be precise. There was so much ambiguity around me — or so it seemed to me.

Fortunately, everyone there also understood that every new person encountered this bewildering place. They didn't expect me to understand it all immediately, and they were gracious enough to say so and help when it seemed important to do so. As time went by, I slowly found that I was functioning more and more effectively. I didn't really work at it. I just kept doing things and listening to reactions. After six months, I understood the differences and knew how to deal with them. It wasn't a conscious learning. It was more like letting the ambiguities sit for a while and settle as more and more experience was gained. I placed no demands on my mind to clarify but rather let my mind play with what it was learning in its own time. (This is the same principle as relaxing to understand a heavily accented speaker or a scene from *King Lear*.)

When I encounter something totally new, something that challenges every assumption I am aware of, something that seems paradoxical, I have learned to let my mind play. 'Playing' means to open my mind to more and more imagination and observation so that the possibilities of this new thing bubble up. I call this letting my mind play with the ideas, for 'play' is exactly what the mind is doing.

In the state of allowing the mind to play, I have to remove boundaries that may exist, or let them be permeable for a time. I have to be willing to sit in an ambiguous place, where the horizon seems tilted, gravity seems foreign, where there are no reference points that allow me to feel safe. I feel as if I am in an unknown place with no way home. This is the place where the mind can explore and discover new emergent ideas. This is the place or the time when complex relationships are sorted out and rewoven into new understandings, a place where new connections are made.

Terrence Gargiulo, prolific author and consultant, says the same thing in different words, "It is the stillness when the real work is going on. We're not aware of what is going on. Yet the pieces are being put together. ...We play in this liminal space."

Kat Pearl, a teacher in the Waldorf tradition and a human being of extraordinary insightfulness, expresses herself this way. "I am clearer when I keep my meditation practice going. It's important to hear my inner intuition." To her the inner intuition is where things have been put together.

About Play

If you are feeling anxious about letting your mind go—which is sort of what letting it play is all about—here is some research that will help you feel more comfortable about the 'play approach'.

In his paper "Are You Working Too Hard?" Benson introduces the results of research that show that individual efficiency is enhanced with pressure up to a certain point, at which time, the pressure actually induces a decrease in efficiency. "Stress is a physiological response to any change, whether good or bad, that alerts the adaptive fight-or-flight response in the brain and the body."[18] When we are exposed to excessively long periods of the fight-or-flight response, the pressure on us becomes too great, and our system is flooded with the hormones epinephrine, norepinephrine, and cortisol. These cause blood pressure to rise and the heart rate and brain activity to increase, effects that are

---

[18] Herbert Benson, "Are You Working Too Hard?" *Harvard Business Review*, November 2005, P. 54.

very deleterious over time. His recommendation is to take a moment and completely let go of the problem. When we are able to do this, the "brain actually rearranges itself so that the hemispheres communicate better. Then the brain is better able to solve the problem."

Feel better about letting the mind play?

On Playing Around

"Flights of fancy are the most practical work of enterprise these days." - Tom Peters

Why does 'play' find a place in this book? Why should play be one of the foundational concepts on which an approach to keeping your knowledge fresh is built? Let me take a playful way to show you that play is an active part of some very powerful minds.

"Imagination is more important than knowledge," said Einstein. He understood how to let his mind play and explore his imagination. He was known to talk about imagining life on a beam of light while looking back at a clock or dropping a coin in an elevator going down. All ways in which he could explore a subject while not being burdened with existing assumptions, because on the surface his imaginings appeared not to relate to the task at hand. He needed to imagine what it would be like to be on a beam of light in order to allow himself to see other possibilities than those that were already understood. If he were alive today, he might take time to imagine what it would be like to live in a world without petroleum.

Mihaly Csikszentmihalyi, in his book *Creativity*[19], describes the characteristics of creative people as those whose personalities are complex and contain contradictory extremes creating within each individual a 'multitude.' Among his many listed characteristics, creative people have a combination of playfulness and discipline, responsibility and irresponsibility. They are naïve along with being smart. And his list of contradicting qualities goes on.

I love how Csikszentmihalyi uses the language of contradiction. How can people be both responsible and irresponsible? To me, it is the ability to allow their minds to play with ideas. To me, it is like someone who can allow confusion into his mind without caring that it be resolved. Csikszentmihalyi later describes the creative process to include a "period of incubation: during which ideas churn around below the threshold of consciousness." I call this the ability to hold multiple ambiguities, allowing the mind to have time and space to play and sort things out. This is play whether you are interested in being creative or just learning. Play is an essential part of embracing new ideas.

In case you need just a bit more to understand what this concept is about, I would like to suggest a short exercise borrowed from John Kao[20].

---

[19] Mihaly Csikszentmihalyi, " *Creativity: Flow and the Psychology of Discovery and Invention,"Harper Perrenial; 4 Tra edition (May 9, 1997)*

[20] In his book *Jamming*, John Kao describes exercises that help people 'clear their minds.' His purpose is to describe how he helps his students and colleagues to have a 'beginner's mind' ready to learn and explore and play and discover and create. He does this by directing people to think about subjects "not burdened with anxiety—subjects with no connection to the task at hand." P. 46.

Think of a favorite movie scene and take a moment to begin to see it in your mind's eye. As you do this, observe what the scene leads you to think. To help you know what I am asking, here is an example from my own exploration of this exercise.

As I begin, I immediately see the scene from the movie *Apollo 13* where the ground crew is told to make a square peg fit into a round hole using only what is on the spacecraft. (The CO_2 scrubbers in the landing device where they have been living have run out, and the crew must use the scrubbers from the other module if they are to survive to landing.) I see the pile of materials as they are poured onto the big table and the looks of puzzlement from the ground crew. It's an exciting scene, because we know that the astronauts will die if they don't solve the problem, and the pile of stuff looks huge and totally incompatible with the assignment.

Letting my mind move where it wants to, I think about the pile almost like a pile of 'junk.' It looks like nothing that needs to be created. I think about the talents and skills needed to solve the problem for the Apollo crew. These are engineers, but they have only their hands to work with. Perhaps there is one among them who is used to working with his hands. Now, I am thinking about how organizations often ignore the unexpected talent or even the mass of talents and skills sitting in their meetings, do they know them all? Do I know all of mine? That's amazing! Do I know all of mine? Wow, I'm in a different place!

Take a minute right now and visualize the movie scene of your choice and record the thoughts that flow into your mind. Don't edit them; let them flow. Open a fresh page in your journal (or other tool) to record your thoughts.

Are you in a different place?

When Kao does this with his students, he describes how they come out of this session transformed. They are in a playful, creative state that he calls 'jamming.' Do this the next time you are in the midst of a problem. Do you feel the change in the way you approach the problem? Let your mind have time to play with those ambiguities it encounters every day.

Boundaries Help Harvest the Insights of Ambiguity

Play in the mind needs to be free of boundaries. When you begin to articulate conclusions, boundaries become useful again. But they may be new boundaries—the joy of allowing the mind to play is that the need for new boundaries may be discovered. Once defined, these new boundaries provide the comfort of knowing where you are and how to get home. And while your mind will return from 'play' to work again, you will bring this new awareness of ambiguity with you. You will never forget the insights gained through the experience. With practice, the ability to hold ambiguity increases.

At this point, you are likely saying, "But what about the container that I defined for myself at the beginning of this book? How can I remove boundaries to let my mind play, when I know that boundaries are needed?" They are both necessary—the boundaries and the ambiguity that demands the boundaries move.

Setting the container for your learning is important for all the reasons noted in Chapter 2. But boundaries were never intended to be permanent. When we are learning new ideas that challenge our assumptions to the point that we encounter ambiguity, we must open the boundaries for the mind to play at will with the new learning. Think of it as being like a Zen koan,[21] functioning in the realm of intuition rather than rational thought.

If this sounds a bit frightening, consider what happens when there is space between two niches in an eco-system. This is precisely where life really takes off. New species are born, populations explode until they are once again brought into balance and the space is filled. Imagine the learning that can occur if you let your mind explore these spaces between the boundaries.

I asked my interview subjects to reflect on ambiguity, and was delighted to learn that most welcome it as essential to their learning approach.

Ralph Scorza is a scientist working in the genetics of fruit trees. He is a master at finding himself in ambiguous spaces. He says, "When things are in apparent conflict, or exclude each other yet both have validity, it gives me an idea there is something important there in the space in between. And that's where I look."

Playwright and director Christopher Heimann confirms this perception when he says, "To watch something ambiguous is much more thrilling for an audience than to watch something that is really clear cut." He explains it this way. "You can carry [opposites] in you. It applies to everything really in art. You say this character is good or this one's bad...that's just boring. People have the capacity to be both. If you play this guy as a bad guy and this one as a good guy, you get cartoon characters. If you can

---

[21] from Wikipedia: A **koan** (pronounced /ko.an/) is a story, dialog, question, or statement in the history and lore of Chan (Zen) Buddhism, generally containing aspects that are inaccessible to rational understanding, yet that may be accessible to intuition. A famous koan is, "Two hands clap and there is a sound; what is the sound of one hand?" (oral tradition, attributed to Hakuin Ekaku, 1686-1769, considered a reviver of the koan tradition in Japan).

tolerate that people who have done wonderful things also have had times where they've done awful things, or vice versa, you get something that is so much more human."

Learning coach Claudia L'Amoreaux says that the root of the word ambiguity means to wander about and around in the root. "Part of the mystery of learning is about the wandering part of it. … I have learned to trust my gut as I'm wandering in the new content. At a certain point, it starts to resolve into some understanding. I sit with the ambiguity and even appreciate it," she says.

When he needs inspiration, Pedro Catarino, surgeon, "spends a lot of time in the library – just to clear my mind and pick up books, especially old ones. They help me relax and are very enjoyable. Sometimes I come across something unexpected and learn something new. For example, looking at writing on kidney dialysis machines [which predated the heart lung machine.] I would never have done so through an electronic search. It's the browsing that allowed me to explore unexpected places."

When a choice between options must be made, manufacturer, Rodger Whipple, "does some analysis, thinking, and discussion…. We may even construct an experiment to give a sense of the best shot to make a decision. Given our size [a small manufacturing plant], we're never sure before we make the decision. So we find evidence through literature searches, similar situations, evidence, test, and we make a decision based on that." Even in manufacturing, life remains ambiguous after research.

Likewise, in her research in medicine, Cait Cusack says, "We gather all the data points we have, hold a face to face meeting, and we say that we need help deciding on what data to use... And when we don't have data we trust… we conduct three rounds of estimates. We get an average with a standard deviation model to make a decision." Life remains ambiguous even in the laboratory.

Ambiguity is not to be feared. It is a signal that there is something more to be learned; there is some new ground that may show yet another option. There is adventure to be had in exploring the white space, and the path home is always there even if we choose to take another. Diving deep can lead to such treasure.

Exploring the Lessons Learned

We learn everyday—what foods we like best, how to drive the shortest route successfully, why the boss is always asking the same question, who is an effective source of information, when to begin dinner in time for the crew to come in to eat. We are amazing creatures. We learn so many lessons that we rarely are aware of all we know.

Organizations often learn lessons and then forget them because the lesson was never articulated. By working with this book, you have just invested a fair amount of time exploring your knowledge strengths and needs, sources, techniques for learning and approaches that support your creative side. You have learned how to learn a bit more. (You may not be aware of it, but you have been working through a whole learning process that models good learning techniques.)

Don't waste your time invested so far, as many organizations do. Take time now to really deepen your learning by thinking about and articulating what you have learned.

Exploring the Lessons Learned: Preparatory Exercises

This exercise is a "brain warm-up." Categorize the following list of items: use any categories that seem logical to you to make sense of the list.

House	Bedroom	Slippers
Kitchen	TV	Fox
Cardinal	Sexy	Knight
Conversation	Members	Office
Paper	Screen	Gown
Tango	Table	Fish
Hat	Gold	Silver
Bridge	Puzzle	Text message
Delicious	Finch	Carpet

Once you have finished categorizing them, start again and create a new and different set of categories into which you will sort the same words. This is not as easy as it sounds, and as a result is very much worth the effort to do.

Exploring the Lessons Learned: Action Exercises

With each chapter, I've encouraged you to record your thoughts about lessons learned and possible options for future action. Now it's time to make use of the notes you've taken along the way.

Gather up all of your notes from the "Record and reflect" sections of the previous chapters. Whether you chose to use a spiral bound journal, a notebook, a computer program, a blog or some other tool, have it handy for easy reference

Read through the lessons learned and see if they group themselves into broader lessons. Take your time, as this is an important step. What are you learning from all of these activities? Where have you found conflicts or ambiguities? Is there 'white space' anywhere? Explore the white spaces—and if you find none, look deeper.

Once you have finished grouping your lessons learned into broader lessons, start again and see if you can find a new and different set of categories for the same lessons (which the warm-up exercise prepared you to do). It's a rare situation in which one categorization scheme alone serves the richness of the information being categorized. By asking you to consider additional groupings, I invite you to the place of ambiguity, the 'both/and' world where the sweet fresh water of new knowledge flows.

Your list might become quite long—that's a good thing. The more lessons are on your list, the better. This is not the time to limit the insights you have gained.

Expected Results/Outcomes

Make a list of lessons learned. Be sure to write them in full sentences. In some cases, you may even wish to write a short paragraph about them so that you can use this activity to explore what the lessons learned mean to you. Don't shortchange yourself on this process. This is where you will find gold.

Record and Reflect

After you have given sufficient time to the exercises, sit down with the lists of lessons learned (which should consist of sentences or paragraphs). Prioritize the list. Which are the lessons that have the greatest leverage to help you achieve your objectives or life goals? Remember, not all of them have to be career related.

Figure 6.2: Excerpts from Madelyn's Journal

After looking at the various lessons I noted in each chapter, I challenged myself to find another organization than the chapter headings. I had to keep telling myself there was another way to look at it and finally I found it. Once I did this, the overarching lessons sprang into life. Here are the new categories and what I learned...

Characteristics clients value
Larger lesson: Riding the current is the only option if I want to remain of value to my clients.

Actions that I do to remain current
Larger lesson: I can handle a few more actions to enhance keeping fresh...

Characteristics of my environment
Larger lesson: I must find Practice Partners (more than one or two) who will be willing to learn with me...

Possible Options

Consider how you might begin to act on the list of lessons you've prioritized. What would following through look like? Who would be involved? Perhaps it's time to engage others in conversation about the broader lessons and insights you've drawn from your work.

Now is a good time to get together with your Accompanier, Practice Partner, and/or fellow seekers. As you describe your lessons to others, you help yourself absorb what you are learning, and test how well you have absorbed it. After listening to you, their observations may reveal an angle you've overlooked. This is how conversation works to help you ride the current.

Possible Actions: What Others Have Said About Deciding to Dive Deep

- Avoid hardened opinions; keep yourself flexible and open enough to change your mind
- Join only the most essential societies of your profession and then become active in them
- Propose to speak at conferences in order to sharpen your understanding of a topic and to meet experts not known to you today
- Explore Wikipedia to see what is already available; open up a new topic area where you begin the discussion and monitor regularly
- Set aside time for journaling lessons learned
- Take time to meditate – time for yourself and time for silence
- Organize an informal symposium (perhaps over lunch) where a knotty problem is put before it

- Explore the value of using Open Space Technology[22] for bringing lots of issues out for discussion
- Create a file just for quotations from articles that retain full references and is organized by major topic.
- Seek and read good fiction
- Plan a trip to a museum, city, conference, or event to which you have never gone
- Journal or blog every day on what you have learned and/or observed
- Remain open to new studies and information even if you think you know it already
- Take on an assignment that you know will test your knowledge to the limits (take care that it is one that will permit lower performance during the learning phase)

 Lessons Learned

This is a good moment to review the self-assessment tool provided in Chapter 1. Are there chapters you have yet to work with? If you have not been working through the book sequentially, what chapter is right for you to move to next? Be sure to revisit the exercises in this chapter when you have completed all preceding chapters. You may discover a new treasure of lessons learned as your knowledge about your own knowledge-seeking grows richer.

---

[22] Open Space Technology is a way to enable a large or small group of people to self-manage a conversation of a complex nature and come to conclusions. It was designed by Harrison Owen.

Riding the Current

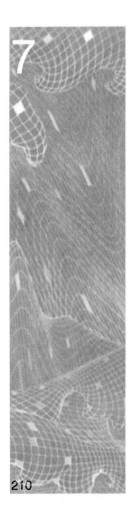

Taking Charge: Deciding What to Do

Dorothy has to do everything the hard way. When I brought out a puzzle, Dorothy said that I should put the cover of the box away. "You don't want to have a picture handy. It will make it too easy to do," she said. As I began gathering together the edge pieces of the puzzle, Dorothy said, "Why begin there? You should do a round puzzle, then you wouldn't have pieces with a clear edge."

I ignored my friend's suggestions and continued working the puzzle. I began assembling the edge. Then I gathered pieces of similar color or pattern and put together small sections of the puzzle. Every now and then, I would see a piece among those not yet fitted, pick it up, and put it exactly where it belonged. I enjoyed those moments, but I also knew that they only happened because I had been preparing for the opportunity by doing the puzzle in small segments. Checking the picture on the box cover

The Accompanier's Role: Explore Links to the Larger Goals

Assuming the person you are accompanying has informed you of what he is doing and perhaps asked for some help along the way, this is a good time to help his decision-making by affirming your support of this work. Support is your primary role now. Getting directly involved in the individual's decision making should be by invitation only. If he asks, respond thoughtfully.

If you have made this work an assignment, this step is likely to create a deliverable you have requested or required. If so, you decide how you want to be involved, but make it clear right at the beginning of the process, not at this stage. In this way, the learner is prepared for your expectation of a deliverable.

Assuming the learner has finished defining his intended actions —with you or not—and chooses to share them with you, perhaps as part of his request for some means to enhance his learning (taking a course, attendance at a conference, a new assignment), give him your thoughtful attention.

- Listen to his intended actions or approach as if your work depended on it.
- Ask questions to make sure you understand the approach and how the individual came to his decisions.
- Be honest as to whether you can see the linkage to the larger picture of the industry, field, or organizational goals.
- If you can see the linkage, seek ways you can support the achievement of the individual's intended actions.
- If you are his boss, even if the budget won't support any activity directly, consider options that might lead to his achievement. The following story describes such a situation, and a creative response to a limited budget.

One of the most common complaints that staff members have about keeping current is the inability of the organization to send them to conferences in their field. Budget is the usual excuse. Han was disappointed when conference fees were out of reach. Frustrated by the lack of funds herself, the manager suggested that Han write a proposal to speak at the conference. She even offered to give Han time to do this writing. When the proposal was accepted, the cost was reduced to travel only, and the budget allowed for this. More importantly, Han claimed that preparing the proposal and the presentation alone was a learning experience. Such encouragements have led to remarkable things!

If you are the learner's boss, another unexpected benefit can occur at annual evaluation time. Annual evaluation exercises typically include a discussion about areas in which the person being evaluated should enhance his knowledge or skills. But it rarely happens this way. What usually comes out of the evaluation on a person's development is the supervisor saying something like, "I'm recommending you for xyz training." When the person being evaluated has developed their own approach for riding the current, you have the opportunity to see that individual's own areas of interest. Building on these guarantees motivation to achievement.

If learning to ride the current was an assignment to a team, here is where the team can be most beneficial to each other. Instead of you playing the role of support, they can support each other. Again, explore this early and make mutual support part of the approach if the team agrees. And, if your team has done this work thoroughly, you will see how their interests serve company goals—essential for offering company resources.

Now, for the writing of the vision story—This is a very personal activity. Your role is to assume the person will do it. Expectation is powerful all by itself.

If writing a vision story is part of a team's assignment, they may wish to share their stories with each other. Perhaps this can be part of an exercise where they then create a vision story together. What's important is that the decision to do so is up to them.

periodically, I finished the puzzle in several sittings over the weekend. Dorothy continued her comments about my techniques and how they had made the puzzle easier to put together. In a burst of frustration with my friend's unhelpful comments and obvious misperception of the purpose of putting a puzzle together, I exclaimed, "Is the puzzle finished? Yes! Did I have a good time? Yes!"

Deciding what to do sometimes feels like putting together a big jigsaw puzzle. At first there is total chaos. Slowly, with a bit of patience, the pieces come together. As they do so, there are moments of sheer brilliance, and a picture — a plan of action — appears.

But planning is not about brilliance, it is about creating the sequence of steps, enjoying the sense of completion when it is ready, and then getting on with it. To return to our metaphor of a voyage in search of treasure, planning is about thoughtfully stocking supplies for the journey, recruiting the crew, and selecting the right vessel in which to go forward. I've gone very light on 'planning' as a component of your approach to riding the current to keep your knowledge fresh and alive. This is simply because I've seen too many people bog down in planning, never reaching the reward of action.

There are many approaches to putting a plan together, and many resources offering to show you how. From my point of view, how you proceed is entirely up to you. I encourage you to find a planning approach that is enjoyable to you, so that you are most likely to complete the plan.

Rather than dwelling on format or methodology, let me continue to offer insights from my research, work, and personal experience. In talking with people to see how they actually did keep their knowledge fresh, three dimensions seem to guide their strategies.

The first seemed to be the audience for their work—how large the audience was, and how complex or unpredictable the needs of the audience might be. The second dealt with interpersonal interaction. If the individuals' area of focus was one where interpersonal interaction is important, their strategies reflected this reality. The third dimension was the rate of information flow. The demands of the individuals' fields include keeping up with a very high volume of new content, demanding efficient strategies for keeping their knowledge fresh.

Consider these examples of how people have addressed these dimensions of audience, interpersonal interaction and inflow of new information. All of them desire to remain fresh in their fields. Some have common emphasis on one dimension over the others, and we'll look at what they have in common. From these examples, you may find some useful ideas, some interesting pieces of your puzzle for creating your own approach.

Challenging Audience? Cast a Wide Net

When the emphasis is on satisfying a broad and changing audience

Politicians and other public officials must cast their nets wide. Those who work for the public are amazing when they take their job seriously to assure their knowledge is fresh. Led by the philosophy of "trust but verify", these three examples show just how broadly they must seek knowledge. No wonder senators have staffs.

There must be a secret to handling multiple sources. Kai Hagen, a County Commissioner in Frederick, Maryland, is a strong researcher when he has a job at hand. He recommends, "Visiting sites, interviewing staff. I read a lot of things, too – magazines, newspapers. For example, I get *Governing* magazine, *MACO* (Maryland Association of Counties), and *NACO* (National Association of Counties), a lot of magazines on land use, parks and recreation, agricultural preservation. The *Governing* magazine covers a lot of topics from budgets to administration to copying to GIS programs, all of the things a county can use to run more efficiently and more effectively. I talk to people, go to conferences (I get some benefit from that)... I use the Internet constantly for a little bit of everything—as a source of information, documents, research, scientific reports, experience in other communities, public reactions, policy statements. If I'm interested in a particular policy, I can go find twenty or thirty different versions of the same idea in different places and see what's working and what hasn't. I can download the actual ordinances, read through some of the newspaper articles, look at some of the commentary. Maybe, I'll even email or call some of the key players involved and ask them how it works for them. This can lead to this kind of personal follow up. It's always been my nature to do that." Later in the interview, Kai reveals that he is a very, very fast reader.

Jan Gardner, also a County Commissioner in Frederick, chooses another strategy. Serving the same wide audience, she has a slightly different emphasis in her approach to keeping her knowledge fresh. "It's hard to stay current because everything changes so quickly... I go back to conversation with other people in like jobs... You can cut through all the information and not have to do the research twice. You'll learn a lot more from others' actual experience than just reading about it... You learn from the dialogue. You get one answer and you can ask, "What comes next?" You just can't do that by reading it on the Internet or in a manual."

Is there a third way? Maryland State Representative, Rick Weldon, uses many sources. "Oh, goodness…I'm an NPR-aholic, C-SPAN junkie…if I'm working in my office in downtown Brunswick, National Public Radio is on the radio, C-SPAN or the county government TV channel is on in the background. Of course there are times when it becomes white noise… It requires a good ear to listen for certain things that are important. I am an active participant in blog sites, and I have found that to be incredibly important, more so than I ever thought they would be… I keep [browser] windows open while I'm working, to be able to pop onto the Frederick News Post forum or the Baltimore Sun forum just to see what people are talking about… Public officials don't realize they are missing a great opportunity… people who pay attention to these issues have strong feelings and aren't necessarily comfortable showing up at a public meeting or writing a letter to an editor, but they are bursting at the seams to share thoughts on their blogs." Rick tells me he always identifies himself when he adds a blog comment—making every communication part of his dialogue with his audience.

Perfecting the Interpersonal Interaction

When interpersonal interaction is what you sell

Consultants find they must not just keep current on many fronts, they must be out in front of their clients on those topics. Their challenge is to retain perspective, and continually transform themselves in response to the trends in the world, in order to remain valuable to their clients.

What role does the stock market play in depth psychology? Katherine Grace Morris is a specialist in depth psychology. Her strategy for riding the current includes reading, attending workshops, working in the field and developing her own material. But she also has participated for over six years with a group that meets regularly to discuss dreams. (Katharine understands that important 'play' happens when the mind is asleep. For more on the importance of play, see Chapter 6.) "Then there is film…and literature that is not directly related to my field. But depth psychology invites the whole world into [consideration.] We are looking at archetypal patterns, so the other area of interest I have is in economics, and in particular the stock market. It's fascinating to me both from a purely monetary point of view but also to see the archetypal pattern in the stock market, because it's completely driven and influenced by human behavior, regardless of all the different [computer-based] programs that they use… There's beauty, there's creativity, there's wisdom, there's war."

It has to be a two-way street for Mary Alice Arthur, a strong and effective consultant. She relies on her network of colleagues and friends. "I'm into talking with people. This interaction… is how I stay fresh. I ring people and start talking. I also read stuff, and when I see email that has value, I forward everywhere. I have begun to realize that I find what I need just about the time I need it."

In consulting, the need for keeping fresh and alive is paramount. Terrence Gargiulo says, "I am finding community for now [is essential.] And I always want to explore for myself. I have a hunger for reading. I read two books at a time; web sites; conversations, especially when the participants are speaking from the heart. I need to be with people like this and have them in my life, because they are also molding and transforming themselves… I never tire of exploring."

Yvette Hyater-Adams, also a consultant, takes a different approach. She focuses on books, journals, and professional associations. Of course, the Internet is part of her strategy as well. "I go to lots of workshops, too, and professional certification programs. The big association I belong to is NTL [National

Training Laboratories] for the Applied Behavioral Sciences. ...I'm also a member of the Association of Humanistic Psychology especially for their different trainings...I'm interested in a lot of the creative arts therapy stuff. The International Coaching Federation (ICF) and that's more of a narrative coaching type thing..." Yvette regularly reads the *Journal of Poetry Therapy, Journal of Humanistic Psychology*, and *Behavioral Sciences Journal*. She occasionally procures a copy of The Journal for Evidence Based Coaching from the U.K. "I read *Harvard Business Review* and get a lot of their cases, too," says Yvette.

Keep in mind that consultants who wish to remain valuable to clients—old and new—must morph themselves constantly to distinguish themselves from others. It's quite a challenge.

When the emphasis is listening and observation

For some individuals, understanding personal reactions and interpersonal interactions is essential. Here, listening and observation (including of oneself) become important. Artists live in a different and very real world that demands interaction and constant observation.

Christopher Heimann, the director and playwright, approaches keeping fresh in a way that allows someone working in an area that includes ancient principles to stay in touch with the latest relevant scientific research. "On the one hand I like that there's a timelessness about the theater...how can two people connect, how do you connect together as a group, how can you work on a common impulse, how do you connect with your imagination and find flow? I think these are pretty timeless things... people have dealt with them for a long time. So in that sense, I keep current by not assuming that because something worked last week with one type of person that it won't necessarily work again this week. One way to keep current is to be more interested in the person I'm with rather than my own technique. I stay open to questioning my own technique."

Christopher doesn't stop there. He goes on to say, "I'm really interested in neuroscience and discoveries about the functioning of the brain. ... There are ways of objectifying things that up until now could only be intuitively felt. And because acting is so much about states of mind and getting into a certain zone... about confidence and whether we're at ease. Are there direct ways of affecting that?... [There is a] university professor in London who does experiments with brain waves... [We are exploring] possible collaboration between his university and our acting department... In some ways, it's about keeping current in the field of science and a mixture of ancient stuff." Notice how Christopher's approach keeps coming back to the human interaction and how to observe this better.

Dena Hawes is an artist who creates objects instead of plays. In this role, her strategy for keeping her knowledge fresh also uses observation and the interaction with colleagues. She says, "Yes, I read books on art—mostly art of the twentieth century, 1970 to current. But my preferred strategy is observing different cities—the art scene in each. So, when I visit a city, I see as much as I can. There are radically different things happening from Washington to New York to LA. I went to the futurism show at the Corcoran. They were drawing these buildings—imaginary buildings—that can now be built. It was fascinating. It's one of my favorite things to do—go observing. Now, in [my work in] conflict resolution, I read a lot, go to lectures, check out current books. I try to stay up to date, but I read a lot of older books, too. They give you a foundation [of] the theories and how they are still relevant and still apply to certain kinds of conflict." And when Dena goes 'observing', she often does it with others who are interested in art. "When we get together, we go to experimental galleries and talk about it and exchange ideas. We have deep conversations. These colleagues are the ones who really keep me current," she says.

When working with human potential

Others who work with human potential also focus on this second dimension of keeping knowledge fresh—the emphasis on interpersonal interaction.

When a congregation is your main client, listening is at the top of the list of strategies. Unitarian minister Elaine Peresluha says, "First, I listen. That word encompasses it all. I listen to myself, the media, the news, my heart, what other people are telling me, my colleagues, the unconscious rumblings that happen. It's a perception thing. Perceiving that people are content, sad, worried, afraid, anxious, feeling the community and the level of 'disgruntledness' in whatever community I am working in... I have to have my antenna up all the time. It is perceptual, intellectual, spiritual. So, I keep listening. Second, I read—journals, newsletters, current books, other churches' newsletters, my mail. I use the Internet. If there's a particular topic I want more information on, or I hear something that I think, 'ooh, what's that about,' I might Google it and see what comes up just to broaden my understanding... The Internet is a huge resource. Third, I have monthly and weekly meetings with colleagues. My relationships are very important to my staying current. The conversations that we have, and the regularity of knowing I am not alone." Elaine is interacting with the authors of many types of material, as well as with her colleagues, to ride the current.

When you're a coach, you focus on the work of those being coached. It's easy to assume that if you are the coach, it's because you are an expert in the subject. Yet, effective coaches, ones that are always bringing something new to the table, are ones that are constantly observing their own work in relation to the individuals being coached. Testing, observing, reflecting to see what works best with an individual and what techniques have a breadth of impact across many, characterize their strategy for keeping fresh. The content and expertise of the subject is necessary but not sufficient for a coach. Howard Milner, voice coach, says he keeps himself fresh and alive "through my work. Simple as that, really." And Howard is doing this with keen, highly refined observation skills.

College professors may appear to have a great advantage because of their positions in learning institutions with colleagues ready at hand, yet creative strategies to increase interpersonal interactions can add real benefits. In the experience of Aram Karapetyan, a university professor in Armenia, we find an example of how theoretical knowledge is kept fresh through strategic involvement in its application. He uses strategies for keeping his knowledge fresh that reflect his position and location in Armenia. He says, "I learn through study and application. I have three projects with three U.S. universities: California, Arizona, and New Jersey. I am teaching in all three programs. Also, I work in leading specialists by teaching from their books; and also presenting to the author. I also design project work as a local expert together with an international expert." Without his interpersonal interactions, Aram would lose much of the applied knowledge that keeps his theoretical work at the leading edge.

Staying Abreast in a Fast Flow

When keeping up with a very high volume of content

High volume calls for techniques that bring efficiency to the strategies of *focus, technology, and discipline*.

Those in the arenas of science and technology use their own areas of expertise to guide how they keep their knowledge fresh and alive. They must be efficient about it and technology tends to play a major but not the only role.

Ralph Scorza, a scientist, is scientific about his means of keeping his knowledge fresh (or as he has calls it, 'adequate'). "I do this with: (1) literature searches with keywords, (2) targeted conferences. Plus I also know I need information from 'left field,' so I go to unusual conferences or very broad conferences, thus it is a mix. (3) Another source is colleagues who reference papers. (I have good communication with colleagues.) I ask a lot of questions [in an effort to be totally] honest about not knowing it all. I also ask people to send the paper. (4) I invite speakers to come to speak at the laboratory. (5) I learned very early, I read three parts of any paper: Ninety percent of the time, I read the title, thus what's the punch-line in the paper; Fifty percent of the abstracts which has to tell it all; Ten percent of papers but only the discussion portion."

Manufacturing requires a scientific view of keeping knowledge fresh, too. Engineer Rodger Whipple says, "I read engineering trade magazines; market magazines, general technical magazines, e.g., *NASA Technical Briefs*, general *Technology*, *Radiation Curing*; also magazines in similar industries, e.g., appliance industry which also uses small heaters, small fans. We don't get enough time to get to engineering libraries for serious engineering searches unless we are working on a particular project. Then, I go to Madison to search engineering. We also go to the field and look at competitors' installations/equipment. This is a bit harder to do because we can't just go and buy some. We find someone with a competitor's equipment, go to the plant, and, with permission, we poke at the equipment. This drives us all to make better products. Also, we listen to our customer's comments, needs, how they are using their equipment/printing, and what they want. In the field, we can also see problems that operators have in using our equipment."

Computer specialist, Wayne Salamon, is straightforward. "I use IEEE (Institute of Electrical and Electronics Engineers) and my own research. I use the Internet and the web (which are different from each other.)" Moreover, with open source, a new arena for keeping fresh is available. "There are all levels of experience and background. They point to new areas. We learn different ways to solve problems. They are different kinds of colleagues. We never meet, yet this is serious software."

Claudia L'Amoreaux is a learning expert, but her use of technology is paramount today to her strategy for keeping her knowledge fresh. "I get 100's of emails and blogs from colleagues each day. They filter through the most important information and point me to articles in or on blogs or places in 3D web. Also, I have dialogues between people. I attend conferences even within the 3D web. ... I set myself the task of being the eyes and ears for other people as they are for me. I read the paper, different sets of magazines. For example, I read in *Business Week* about a father/son steel business in Japan which gave me ideas even though from an unexpected source. I scan the local Bay Area paper since it is 'Silicon Valley Central.' Lots of businesses in the area are relevant to my work. I also read the *Economist* sometimes because it gives me the international perspective." Claudia goes on to say, "There is much communication flowing; you couldn't meet directly. But we do meet occasionally 'in world'—in the networked world as avatars; and 'in person' which is really special because no one has enough time to do all we want. Also, my network is all around the world, so I must use virtual... I am inventing a way we can meet virtually yet bring more of our 'person' to the session through avatars."

Economist Louise Fox works in the international arena, yet she is very focused in her research. "I try to be clear about what I am going to do and be clear that the topic is probably of high value. For a conference, I go to known speakers who move the field forward. I check to see there is evidence I will be getting something new. I read articles and summaries of publications."

When you work in a very old field

As a master carpenter, Raymond Douherty says, "I focus on something within my field. I love carpentry. Wood is my passion. It's a wonderful ability to have. I think out of all the trades, it has the widest scope. It covers so much. From a wedge that holds a door, to dishes, to building a house, to making art... I read to find new ideas—a few magazines and trade magazines."

These are just a few of the strategies that people have shared with me. I hope that at least one of them inspired you, gave you some new ideas or confirmed your thinking. The variety of strategies reflects the needs of each profession and the container set to support the goal. Notice how some are very focused while others range far even as their topics range far.

Taking Charge: To Plan or Not to Plan

When you begin something new, do you first plan or do you jump in or something in between? As you have been going through this book, you have been asked to write lessons and possible actions. Perhaps you have already begun to use new learning strategies as a result of reading this book. Perhaps you are still thinking about it. Now, it is time to decide what to do with all these possibilities.

Some people would take all of them, prioritize them, and start at the top. Others might look at them and get completely discombobulated. More are likely to pick and choose the ones that look most productive (or easiest, depending on perspective) and start there. And others still will say they already have an approach and will refine it based on what they have considered.

How you decide what you will do next is up to you and what you know about yourself and your willingness to follow through.

How you attack this list of options that you have created is up to you. I know that for me the next step is to add refinements to my current approach. Anything new has to fit into what I already do and must be easy and short enough to remember. I'll be presenting my approach later on in the chapter.

Now, if you are thinking that you would like to plan, but where is there time to plan, there is another way to think about this. Time is not the limiting factor of putting a plan together. When I asked people for any wish they would want to help them keep their knowledge fresh, only ten percent asked for more time. Most asked for more face to face conversations (30%). Of the others, they asked for more resources such as staff, money for technology, a laboratory (20%), an improved environment where keeping knowledge fresh was more valued and supported by management (20%), or enhanced mental capabilities (20%).

Fresh from her A-level exams, Laura Woods-Nokes said, "I would like to be able to put my forehead on a book, and learn everything, understand it, and retain it." A wish, I'm sure we would all appreciate being granted.

Claudia L'Amoreaux is masterful at attacking this desire for time. To her, she sees her role as 'conjuring time.' She challenged me to do this once, and I was amazed. 'Conjuring time' meant that I had to be clear about what time I wanted, and then keeping that focus as I rearranged other priorities to allow for it. The amazing thing was that I found the time. It was as if my focusing on a single window helped open it.

So, if you are by nature a planner, make planning your focus, to help that window open for you. If you are not a planner, then consider how you might get the return on your investment thus far in this book. It can only happen if you take some action. And if you are one of those who feels slightly overwhelmed by what you have thought of doing, take a deep breath and find the most simple, easiest, fastest idea to do and begin there. The longest journey begins with the first step.

Deciding What to Do: Preparatory Exercises

Read through the following options and pick the one that appeals to you the most. Then do it.

- Write a story about how you planned (or didn't plan) something that worked out in the end.
- Think of the most complex project you ever worked on. Write down how you attacked the project and got it done.
- Think of a trip you took and write down both the mishaps and serendipitous events that occurred during the trip. Write down why you think each mishap or serendipity occurred.
- Write a story about how your coach taught you the plays in football and how the plays helped during the game.
- Think about how you approach a new recipe to be served at your next dinner party.

Whichever option you choose, be as clear as you can in the story you write.

Deciding What to Do: Action Exercises

If you have completed the work of the previous six chapters, you have gained great insights into what you are known for, your strengths, the way in which you learn best, and what makes you most creative in using what you know.

Now is the time for you to look at your desires for your work and career (or your life). Where can you build on your knowledge strengths, where should you shore up your knowledge, where would you like to improve? Where can you be more efficient in your regular information gathering, and where can you further develop your use of what you know? The following questions will help you reflect on what you have just learned. Answer one or more of the questions using the notes from the 'Record and Reflect' sections in previous chapters.

- What did you learn in each of the exercises? Write down what was surprising to you.
- Of what you learned (new or otherwise), what was most useful to you and why?
- For each of the sections of inquiry, what questions did you find the most useful? Why?
- For each of the sections of inquiry, what questions would you add?
- What kind of information do you need to set the right priorities about what you should spend time learning about, staying current, keeping fresh, or discovering? Do you have that information now? (If you don't, take some time and go get it.)
- What insights did you gain through the exercise on learning? How can they serve your decision for keeping your knowledge fresh?
- If you were a manager, how might you use this knowledge for yourself? If you are helping to develop staff, how might you use this knowledge for or with your staff?

You are now ready to decide on actions.

If You Prefer Not to Plan

If you feel that a plan is simply overkill on this topic, then there are only two things that might help at this point. First, think about what you have discovered as you have done the exercises in this book. Sit quietly so that you are able to consider the implications of your discoveries. Sleep on it if you need to. Second, decide the actions you are ready to take to ride the current of knowledge. Write them down if that is helpful. Now, start doing what you have decided to do.

If Planning is Your Preference

You know how to plan a dinner, a conference, a party. The end state is easy to visualize. The tasks required to create that state are not hard to imagine. If you feel concern about omitting a step or performing one incorrectly, it's easy to hit the Internet and find templates and advice for these types of plans. So why should creating a plan for implementing your new learning approach seem daunting?

To help you develop your plan, consider the lists of possible actions and design options presented here. More than one is offered, so that you can choose which approach is closest to your own personal style. And if your style isn't included, create one for yourself. The objective is to move you from gathering insights to making decisions to action.

The easiest plan is simply to list your intended actions. If you choose this approach, I recommend that you challenge yourself to list at least three actions that will move you toward your desires. The most important thing is that you list actions that you can commit yourself to doing.

As you do this, you may find that some of the actions require that your organization play a role. If so, use your plan as a conversation starter with your supervisor or team leader. If you interviewed him or her in the exercises in Chapter 4, this is a great time to show that you have continued working through the exercises since that conversation. Before you meet with your supervisor again, identify why each of your actions support the mission of your organization. Then be sure to mention those mission-supporting actions as you talk. It always helps. If you are not part of an organization, then consider sharing this with your Accompanier. It is sure to stimulate a conversation of value to you.

To help you, I've provided several examples of the

229

form an action plan might take, including a MindMap, a table, and a napkin; see "Some Options for Creating a Plan" in Annex 2 in the Appendix.

Vision Drives the Mission

Whether you plan or not, a vision of the results helps drive the mission. You have come to the last step. You set sail into the unknown of learning about learning. You dove deep, and you returned with insights. Now you need to make the vision of the achievement of your plan as clear as possible. One of the best ways to do so is to write a story about a future time when you have completed your plan. Cast your mind forward a couple of years. Be a reporter—look around, and write about what you are seeing.

Take as much time and space as you wish, but make sure that you write it down. To help you, I've provided a story structure; see "Writing Your Story" in Annex 3 in the Appendix, where you'll find an example to help you understand this story structure. Use the template or not, but write the story down.

Advice to Young People

While you are creating your plan, consider the advice given by those interviewed to young people starting out. That may not be you, but you may be surprised at what could be useful to you even if you are not 'young' or 'starting out.' After all, most of us will have three, four or more careers in our working lives, meaning we will start out in a new venue with some frequency.

I hope that in Table 7.1 you will recognize some actions you have already decided to incorporate, from your work in the earlier chapters.

Table 7.1: Recommendations For Young People or Those in the Midst of Change[23]

Enhance your skills of observation and perception
- Keep an open mind
- Force yourself to take a centrist view so that your mind remains open to new ideas and options
- Don't stay in a bubble
- Look at art and discuss what you have seen
- Develop your skills in observing and perceiving
- Learn how to deal with the rhetoric from others who place demands on you
- Make yourself a deep observer and great noticer
- Be aware of what you are doing in relation to the product—observing all aspects relative to its use
- Spend less time on wasteful things and more time with people
- Be aware at all times

Create a thinking environment for yourself
- Spend more time in nature
- Meditate
- Value yourself enough to give yourself time to be you
- Challenge yourself to go always to the next level
- Don't worry about performing, rather see where you can contribute
- Give each other space but learn how to be there for each other
- Work with people
- Avoid procrastination

Make selection of topics consciously and thoughtfully
- Keep in touch with yourself, your needs, and what inspires you.
- Narrow things down using personal interest as an important guide
- Don't specialize too much even in an area that excites you
- Get into what you are doing
- Be clear about what you are ' bringing to the table'

Connect with people
- Seek out great colleagues; you need a social context
- Find colleagues who speak to your needs
- Talk to lots of people

---

[23] Source: those interviewed

- Network
- Join the professional organization(s) in your area
- Get a good mentor who is willing to invest above average time in you
- Get out of the office
- Don't depend on Internet conversation alone

Be a life long learner
- Don't ever assume that you know enough
- Keep up on current theory
- Go across disciplines
- Never stop learning
- Keep yourself in a continuous learning state

Read, read, read
- Select the key publications, journals and other key sources for your area
- Learn to speed read

Use the Internet
- Set up Google searches early
- Learn how to use and manage all the available tools of the Internet

Accept opportunities
- Say yes to opportunities
- Use experts
- Use the talents you have around you

Cross boundaries
- Cross the boundaries of age, culture, disciplines
- Attend art shows, visit museums, farms, senior centers, zoos.....
- Read a range of materials

✓ Expected Results/Outcomes

At this point, you should have a list of intended actions as well as a vision story to help you visualize what you want to accomplish as a result of your learning approach.

Record and Reflect

List the key events in your approach that surprised you as you made decisions about your intended actions. You won't find the expected 'Possible options' and 'Lessons learned' here because it's decision time now!

Excerpts from Madelyn's journal

In addition, for the last 16 years, I have followed several practices that enabled me to not only remain fresh in my knowledge but to be able to access information when needed.

Covering a lot of ground:

I 'trash' read most books. I read until I have discovered the message of the book, only then do I decide if I am going to read the whole thing...

...I have maintained a database of key articles with key words to allow for quick searching.

...Looking to the future, I am a person who prefers to keep a few things in mind rather than a long plan. Here is....

Guiding objectives	New Intended Actions
Trends I see that are important to me are:	
Growing need to be both efficient and effective in a global economy	Organize web pages in del.icio.us using tags...
Professional: to remain current in the field	
...	Write on the subject
...	Continue to interview; hire a student intern to review literature each summer

Riding the Current

8

234

Looking Back and Looking Forward

A Small Success

Can you really ride the current? Recently I was working with a world-renowned expert in knowledge management to serve one of my clients. I was excited to hear what he had to say about the topic and a bit nervous that he would offer them much more than I could.

As he talked, I realized that his words were different from mine, but his message was one I knew well. Then as he mentioned book after book that our client might find useful in their work, I realized that I was aware of and had read through every book he mentioned but one. To my relief, my new approach of riding the current was working.

It felt good to be able to add to the conversation my specific comments on the material he referenced. The client came away knowing that I was knowledgeable even of the most current publications. I felt the investment I have been making in my plan to ride the current was paying off very well.

There is an excitement about beginning a trip. There is the anticipation of seeing new places, visiting old friends or making new ones, eating good food, being away from the ordinary of life. Even during the trip, there is the anticipation of the next stop, the next event, even the trip home.

At the beginning of this book, we invited you on a journey by asking you to think about your **destination**—what is it that draws you to improving the way you keep yourself fresh. This destination may have remained the same as you proceeded. It may have changed to reflect a greater understanding of the possibilities. In either case, I hope you are now looking forward to your journey with the same enthusiasm that accompanies the beginning of a long-anticipated trip.

We've talked about selecting the **right vessel** that will hold what you need to get to your destination. Does the vessel still feel right or have you already modified it as you discovered new things and more about yourself? Either way, I hope you've made decisions that feel good to you in this moment.

We've talked about **who** you should take along with you—colleagues, Practice Partners, and even an Accompanier. One of the joys I have discovered as I developed this approach is that as you bring them into your exploration, they become friends as well. Your circle of conversations may have widened over the course of your journey thus far. As you continue that circle will widen further, bringing interesting new people into your life. That's another delight to anticipate.

We've given you time to design your **approach**. It can be disciplined reading, or continuous conversations, or careful attention to what is happening around you, something else or some combination. You have learned about your strengths as others see you. Using these, you are the one who decides which approach you will use and to what extent. And if you find it isn't working, you simply switch to another method. Have you added new strategies to your search for current knowledge?

Finally, we invited you to **jump over the edge** of your vessel and dive deep for the knowledge — whether it was specific or ambiguous. Those new strengths on which you have gained insight, coupled with your curiosity, will drive your explorations. Or perhaps you have decided that the best strategy for you is to remain well within your discipline and explore for new knowledge within it. Whichever you choose, let it be right for you.

On this trip, you have likely built a sense of excitement and anticipation of how you will keep yourself more aware of what is going on — riding the current. If you have done the exercises in this book, the question remains how to sustain this commitment to do so on an ongoing basis. How can you sustain the excitement? How can you feel the freshness when you find yourself doing the same things over and over?

The answer is in the discovery of new knowledge. Whether that knowledge takes the shape of broad awareness or in-depth and specific information, it is your treasure. You laid out the reasons for taking this trip in search of it. If your reasons are still valid, remind yourself of them. If they are no longer valid, it's time to think about and discover the new reasons that call to you. Where will the greatest value be returned for your investment of time?

This book has been an exploration of how people take on the task of staying fresh in their fields of interest — how they ride the current to remain aware and, when called, take the conscious plunge into the deep, to find the treasures of knowledge. The most remarkable aspect of this kind of journey is that it can be taken again and again, yet never be dull. It's like drawing from a well over and over again and still bringing up water that is fresh.

Even after a trip around the world, there are still new places to go. Even visiting the old places can carry unexpected surprises. For example, have you ever felt you knew all the best restaurants in a city you have visited? As many times as I have gone to Amsterdam, I am always finding another great restaurant.

On a knowledge journey, new worlds are being created as you travel. Think of it—the potential is infinite. Imagine the joy of finding yourself at the same place and discovering something totally new and exciting. It's almost like imagining that the journey is along the spiral of a nautilus. You are looking in the same direction, but the options are suddenly larger and more spacious. Knowledge seems to work this way. As you understand a question more deeply, when you ask it again, the answer always must be deeper and richer as well.

Some of us know that we are lifelong learners. The simple act of learning is reason enough to ride the current every day of our lives. For others, it is a challenge to find the reason that calls us, the value for investing in staying on board and riding the current. Is it to remain viable in a field or career? Is it to be aware of the latest? Is it to enjoy the satisfaction of uncovering something truly new?

To me one of the greatest joys is that in this act of learning, we each lead ourselves. You are the one who sets your learning goals. You are the one who creates the approach. You are the one who motivates yourself, supports yourself in following it. You are indeed the captain of your Knowledge Seeker.

In all my work as a manager, a coach, a mother, I have never found anyone who was not excited when he or she learned something new and unexpected. It must be part of being human to be curious, to be adventurous, to like being surprised, to seek what lies around the corner, over the waves, down in the depths.

Come ride the current with me.

Annex 1: Conducting the Interviews

See Chapter 4 for context of this annex.

Some of us may never have interviewed another person formally. This short guideline is for them.

To help you in the interview, have the questions (numbered) listed on a separate sheet which I call a *side page*. It is also helpful to have the reason for the interview noted on this side sheet. People like to know why they are doing something before they invest their time. You have a legitimate reason for interviewing them, and they should know it.

Record your **interviews** in a bound notebook of some variety. As you record the responses to the questions in your notebook, do so next to the number of the question or perhaps you prefer to place a key word just before beginning the response. Either will work. Here is an example of what your 'side page' might look like.

Introduction

I appreciate your time in agreeing to be interviewed. My purpose in doing this is to create a plan for myself that will help me focus on the areas where my knowledge can be best put to use or enhanced to be more useful. This interview will last about 30 minutes, but if you want to take more time, I have set that aside. Do you have any questions of me before we begin?

1. Tell me about a time when you decided to come to me for **information/knowledge/know-how**. What was the topic? Are there other topics that you feel I know?

2. Tell me about a time when you came to me for help because you felt I knew something that would be **helpful to you.**

Be sure to put the names of those you interviewed at the top of the page. (I always record the date as well. It seems to help in my memory process.) You'll be surprised at how hard it will become to separate out the notes later if you don't. If you decide to also record the session electronically, this can be a great way to capture even more, but it does take time for a second listening.

Notes can be in the form of phrases that stand out to you as you listen, key words, or thoughts that come to you as you listen (lessons on the fly). In any event, the shorter your notes are, the quicker you need to write down what they mean to you and add that to your lessons learned. Of course, if you have perfect memory, you don't have to worry about that. Most mortals lack this gift, however.

Annex 2: Options for Creating a Plan

See Chapter 7 for context of this annex.

If you have never made an action plan before, here are some simple approaches. Look at the three illustrations and decide if one fits you or suggests what you would prefer to do. They are offered only to give you inspiration. Once inspired, create that plan for riding the current.

A. MindMapping Your Action Plan

MindMapping is all about creating a picture of what you are planning. As illustrated here.

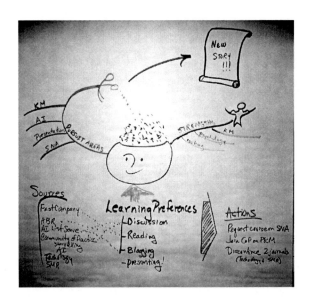

B. An Action Plan in Table Form

If you prefer to do your plan in matrix form with objectives, actions, time tables, and responsibilities, use a form like the one below to develop your plan.

Objectives & Actions	Responsibility	Target Date
Objective 1 Action 1.1 Action 1.2		
Objective 2 Action 2.1 Action 2.2		

C. The Napkin Action Plan

And if you really like things informal – try the 'back-of-a-napkin' approach

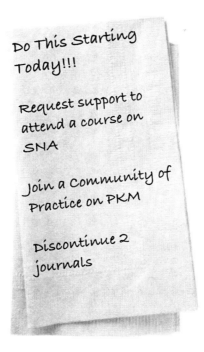

Annex 3: Writing Your Story

See Chapter 7 for context of this annex.

When you are ready to write the story of what things will look like when you implement your plan, the following table presents the structure of story.

One of the best ways is to cast your mind out a couple of years. Be a reporter, look around, and write about what you are seeing. Take as much time and space as you wish, but make sure that you write it down. To help you, here are some questions that stories usually answer. And if you are having problems understanding how these work together, look at the example immediately following the set of questions.

My story[24]

Where and when does your story take place? (LANDSCAPE)

Where does the action begin? (DWELLING PLACE)

Who is a part of this story? (CHARACTERS including their attributes & OBJECTS)

What was the major constraint(s) that led you to take action? (DILEMMA/ PROBLEM)

What did you take action on? What happened as a result? Were there obstacles that you had to surmount? How did you do so? Did anyone help you? (ACTION)

How do things finally resolve? (RESOLUTION)

---

[24] This story structure is from the work of Sparknow, LLC of London.

An example story within the framework

PART	EXPLANATION	EXAMPLE
1. TITLE	Formulate a catchy title to capture the essence of your story.	'The Hare and the Tortoise' – Aesop's Fables
2. LANDSCAPE	Paint a vivid picture of the context including the historical moment and general location in which the events occurred. Build in a sense of significance.	Once upon a time, in a land far, far away...
3. DWELLING PLACE	Pinpoint where the action begins. Include sounds, tastes, smells, feelings to transport your audience.	The race course
4. CHARACTERS including their attributes) & OBJECTS	Introduce the central characters and their roles. For each, identify two key details to give clues about personality.	Tortoise – meek, perseverant. Hare – boastful, arrogant, lazy, greedy. Objects include the sun, the cabbages and the finish line.
5. DILEMMA (which leads to...)	"Everything was normal until suddenly..." What was the unexpected dilemma or conflict?	(For the tortoise) To race or not to race?

PART	EXPLANATION	EXAMPLE
6. ACTION (which includes obstacles, helpers and a turning point)	What happened next? Describe the sequence of events as they unfolded, linked by cause and effect. Identify factors that helped and hindered progress. Clarify the turning point in your drama. Seed in emotion and surprising details, such as plot twists, to keep your audience engaged.	*Tortoise plods slowly on. Hare greedily eats too many cabbages for lunch and falls asleep, believing he will certainly win. He wakes too late (turning point) and can not beat the tortoise. Tortoise's physical slowness was an obstacle, but his determination helped.*
7. RESOLUTION (including the moral or lesson)	How does the story end? What was the change implicit in the story? What can we learn from it?	*Tortoise beats hare, which is reversal of previous fortunes. The moral is "slow and steady wins the race"*

Source: Sparknow, LLC of London.

Related Resources

Learning

Geoff Colvin (2008). <u>Talent Is Overrated: What really separates world-class performers from everybody else</u>, Penguin Books, London.

Matthew B. Crawford (2009). <u>Shop Class as Soulcraft: An Inquiry into the Value of Work</u>. New York: The Penguin Press.

Nancy Kline (1999). <u>Time To Think: Listening To Ignite The Human Mind.</u> London: Ward Lock

Ron Miller (2000). <u>Creating Learning Communities: Models, Resources, and New Ways of Thinking About Teaching and Learning.</u> Brandon, VT: The Foundation for Educational Renewal Inc.

Jeremy Rifkin (2000). <u>The Age of Access: The new culture of hypercapitalism where all of life is a paid-for experience.</u> New York: Penguin Putman

James Surowiecki (2004). <u>The Wisdom of Crowds: Why the Many are Smarter than the Few and How Collective Wisdom Shapes Business, Economies, Societies and Nations.</u> New York: Doubleday

Narrative/Story Telling

Julie Allan, Gerard Fairtlough, & Barbara Heinzen (2001) <u>The Power of the Tail: Using Narratives for Organisational Success.</u> West Sussex, England: John Wiley & Sons

Paul Costello (2008) <u>The Presidential Plot: The map, the story and the conspiracy to elect a president</u>, Storywise, Washington, DC.

Social Construction

Kenneth J. Gergen & Mary Gergen (2004) <u>Social Construction: Entering the Dialog.</u> Chagrin Falls, OH: Taos Institute Publications

Kenneth J. Gergen (2009) <u>Relational Being</u>. New York: Oxford University Press

Kenneth J. Gergen (1994). <u>Realities and Relationships: Sounding in Social Construction.</u> Cambridge, MA: Harvard University Press

Kenneth J. Gergen (2009). <u>An Invitation to Social Construction</u>, Sage Publications Ltd.

Leadership, Community and Spirit

Peter Block ((2008). <u>Community: The STructure of Belonging</u>. San Francisco, CA: Berrett-KoelerPublishers Inc.

Lee G. Bolman & Terrence E. Deal (2001). <u>Leading with Soul: An Uncommon Journey of Spirit.</u> San Francisco, CA: Jossey-Bass

Marcus Buckingham & Donald O. Clifton (2001). <u>Now, Discover Your Strengths:</u> New York: The Free Press

Margaret Wheatley (2005). <u>Finding Our Way: Leadership For an Uncertain Time.</u> San Francisco, CA: Berrett-Koehler Publishers Inc.

Management

Larry Bossidy & Ram Charan (2002). <u>Execution: The Discipline of Getting Things Done.</u> New York: Crown Business

Mick Cope (2000). <u>Know Your Value? Value What You Know: Manage your knowledge and make it pay.</u> London: Pearson Education Limited

W. Timothy Gallwey (2000). <u>The Inner Games of Work.</u> New York: Random House

William Isaacs (1999). <u>Dialogue and The Art of Thinking Together.</u> New York: Doubleday

Gareth Morgan (1993). <u>Imagin•i•zation: New Mindsets for Seeing, Organizing, and Managing.</u> San Francisco, CA: Berrett-Koehler Publishers Inc.

Tom Peters (1994). <u>Crazy Times Call for Crazy Organizations.</u> New York: Vintage Books

Annette Simmons (1999). <u>a safe place for dangerous truths: Using Dialogue to Overcome Fear Distrust at Work.</u> New York: AMA Publications

Appreciative Inquiry

Harlene Anderson, David Cooperrider, Kenneth J. Gergen, Mary Gergen, Sheila McNamee & Diana Whitney (2008) The Appreciative Organization. Chagrin Falls OH: Taos Institute Publications

Frank J. Barrett & Ronald E. Fry (2005) Appreciative Inquiry: A Positive Approach to Building Cooperative Capacity. Chagrin Falls, OH: Taos Institute Publications

Jacqueline Bascobert Kelm (2005). Appreciative Living: The Principles of Appreciative Inquiry in Personal Life. Wake Forest, NC: Venet Publishers

Jacqueline M. Stavros & Cheri B. Torres (2005). Dynamic Relationships: Unleashing the Power of Appreciative Inquiry in Daily Living. Chagrin Falls, Ohio: Taos Institute Publications

Knowledge Management

Raimo P Hamalainen & Esa Saarinen, editors (2004). Systems Intelligence: Discovering a Hidden Competence in Human Action Organisational Life. Helsinki: Helsinki University of Technology

Simon Lelic (2004) Communities of Practice: Lessons from Leading Collaborative Enterprises. London: Ark Group

Mark W. McElroy (2003). The New Knowledge Management: Complexity, Learning and Sustainable Innovation. New York: Butterworth-Heinemann

John Seely Brown & Paul Duguid (2000). The Social Life of Information. Boston MA: Harvard Business School Press

Tojo Thatchenkery & Carol Metzker (2006). Appreciative Intelligence: Seeing the Mighty Oak in the Acorn. San Francisco, CA: Berrett-Koehler Publishers Inc.

Georg Von Krogh, Kazuo Ichijo & Ikujiro Nonaka (2000). Enabling Knowledge Creation: How to Unlock the Mystery of Tacit Knowledge and Release the Power of Innovation. New York: Oxford University Press

Creativity

John Kao (1996) Jamming: The Art and Discipline of Business Creativity. New York: HarperBusiness, HarperCollins

Robert Kegan (1994) In Over Our Heads: The Mental Demands of Modern Life. Cambridge, MA: Harvard University Press

Innovation Learning

Bart Kosko (1993) Fuzzy Thinking: The New Science of Fuzzy Logic. New York: Hyperion

Ikujiro Nonaka & Toshihiro Nishiguchi (2001) Knowledge Emergence: Social, Technical, and Evolutionary Dimensions of Knowledge Creation. New York: Oxford University Press

Michael Schrage (2000) Serious Play: How the Worlds Best Companies Simulate to Innovate. Boston: Harvard Business School Press

Breinigsville, PA USA
29 April 2010
237023BV00005B/2/P